Christ Is All And In All

THE LOCHLAINN SEABROOK COLLECTION

AMERICAN CIVIL WAR
Abraham Lincoln Was a Liberal, Jefferson Davis Was a Conservative: The Missing Key to Understanding the American Civil War
Confederacy 101: Amazing Facts You Never Knew About America's Oldest Political Tradition
Confederate Blood and Treasure: An Interview With Lochlainn Seabrook
Everything You Were Taught About African-Americans and the Civil War is Wrong, Ask a Southerner!
Everything You Were Taught About the Civil War is Wrong, Ask a Southerner!
Give This Book to a Yankee! A Southern Guide to the Civil War For Northerners
Lincoln's War: The Real Cause, the Real Winner, the Real Loser
The Great Yankee Coverup: What the North Doesn't Want You to Know About Lincoln's War!
The Ultimate Civil War Quiz Book: How Much Do You Really Know About America's Most Misunderstood Conflict?
Women in Gray: A Tribute to the Ladies Who Supported the Southern Confederacy

CONFEDERATE MONUMENTS
Confederate Monuments: Why Every American Should Honor Confederate Soldiers and Their Memorials

CONFEDERATE FLAG
Confederate Flag Facts: What Every American Should Know About Dixie's Southern Cross
What the Confederate Flag Means to Me: Americans Speak Out in Defense of Southern Honor, Heritage, and History

SECESSION
All We Ask Is To Be Let Alone: The Southern Secession Fact Book

SLAVERY
Everything You Were Taught About American Slavery is Wrong, Ask a Southerner!
Slavery 101: Amazing Facts You Never Knew About America's "Peculiar Institution"

CHILDREN
Honest Jeff and Dishonest Abe: A Southern Children's Guide to the Civil War
Saddle, Sword, and Gun: A Biography of Nathan Bedford Forrest For Teens

NATHAN BEDFORD FORREST
A Rebel Born: A Defense of Nathan Bedford Forrest - Confederate General, American Legend (winner of the 2011 Jefferson Davis Historical Gold Medal)
A Rebel Born: The Screenplay (film about N. B. Forrest)
Forrest! 99 Reasons to Love Nathan Bedford Forrest
Give 'Em Hell Boys! The Complete Military Correspondence of Nathan Bedford Forrest
I Rode With Forrest! Confederate Soldiers Who Served With the World's Greatest Cavalry Leader
Nathan Bedford Forrest and African-Americans: Yankee Myth, Confederate Fact
Nathan Bedford Forrest and the Battle of Fort Pillow: Yankee Myth, Confederate Fact
Nathan Bedford Forrest and the Ku Klux Klan: Yankee Myth, Confederate Fact
Nathan Bedford Forrest: Southern Hero, American Patriot - Honoring a Confederate Icon and the Old South
Saddle, Sword, and Gun: A Biography of Nathan Bedford Forrest For Teens
The God of War: Nathan Bedford Forrest As He Was Seen By His Contemporaries
The Quotable Nathan Bedford Forrest: Selections From the Writings and Speeches of the Confederacy's Most Brilliant Cavalryman

QUOTABLE SERIES
The Alexander H. Stephens Reader: Excerpts From the Works of a Confederate Founding Father
The Quotable Alexander H. Stephens: Selections From the Writings and Speeches of the Confederacy's First Vice President
The Quotable Jefferson Davis: Selections From the Writings and Speeches of the Confederacy's First President
The Quotable Nathan Bedford Forrest: Selections From the Writings and Speeches of the Confederacy's Most Brilliant Cavalryman
The Quotable Robert E. Lee: Selections From the Writings and Speeches of the South's Most Beloved Civil War General
The Quotable Stonewall Jackson: Selections From the Writings and Speeches of the South's Most Famous General
The Unquotable Abraham Lincoln: The President's Quotes They Don't Want You To Know!

CIVIL WAR BATTLES
Encyclopedia of the Battle of Franklin - A Comprehensive Guide to the Conflict that Changed the Civil War
Nathan Bedford Forrest and the Battle of Fort Pillow: Yankee Myth, Confederate Fact
The Battle of Franklin: Recollections of Confederate and Union Soldiers
The Battle of Nashville: Recollections of Confederate and Union Soldiers
The Battle of Spring Hill: Recollections of Confederate and Union Soldiers

CONSTITUTIONAL HISTORY
The Articles of Confederation Explained: A Clause-by-Clause Study of America's First Constitution
The Constitution of the Confederate States of America Explained: A Clause-by-Clause Study of the South's
    Magna Carta

VICTORIAN CONFEDERATE LITERATURE
Rise Up and Call Them Blessed: Victorian Tributes to the Confederate Soldier, 1861-1901
The God of War: Nathan Bedford Forrest As He Was Seen By His Contemporaries
The Old Rebel: Robert E. Lee As He Was Seen By His Contemporaries
Victorian Confederate Poetry: The Southern Cause in Verse, 1861-1901

ABRAHAM LINCOLN
Abraham Lincoln: The Southern View - Demythologizing America's Sixteenth President
Lincolnology: The Real Abraham Lincoln Revealed in His Own Words - A Study of Lincoln's Suppressed,
    Misinterpreted, and Forgotten Writings and Speeches
Lincoln's War: The Real Cause, the Real Winner, the Real Loser
The Great Impersonator! 99 Reasons to Dislike Abraham Lincoln
The Unholy Crusade: Lincoln's Legacy of Destruction in the American South
The Unquotable Abraham Lincoln: The President's Quotes They Don't Want You To Know!

NATURAL HISTORY
North America's Amazing Mammals: An Encyclopedia for the Whole Family
The Concise Book of Owls: A Guide to Nature's Most Mysterious Birds
The Concise Book of Tigers: A Guide to Nature's Most Remarkable Cats

PARANORMAL
Carnton Plantation Ghost Stories: True Tales of the Unexplained from Tennessee's Most Haunted Civil War
    House!
UFOs and Aliens: The Complete Guidebook

FAMILY HISTORIES
The Blakeneys: An Etymological, Ethnological, and Genealogical Study - Uncovering the Mysterious Origins
    of the Blakeney Family and Name
The Caudills: An Etymological, Ethnological, and Genealogical Study - Exploring the Name and National
    Origins of a European-American Family
The McGavocks of Carnton Plantation: A Southern History - Celebrating One of Dixie's Most Noble
    Confederate Families and Their Tennessee Home

MIND, BODY, SPIRIT
Autobiography of a Non-Yogi: A Scientist's Journey From Hinduism to Christianity (Dr. Amitava Dasgupta,
    with Lochlainn Seabrook)
Britannia Rules: Goddess-Worship in Ancient Anglo-Celtic Society - An Academic Look at the United
    Kingdom's Matricentric Spiritual Past
Christ Is All and In All: Rediscovering Your Divine Nature and the Kingdom Within
Christmas Before Christianity: How the Birthday of the "Sun" Became the Birthday of the "Son"
Jesus and the Gospel of Q: Christ's Pre-Christian Teachings As Recorded in the New Testament
Jesus and the Law of Attraction: The Bible-Based Guide to Creating Perfect Health, Wealth, and Happiness
    Following Christ's Simple Formula
Seabrook's Bible Dictionary of Traditional and Mystical Christian Doctrines
The Bible and the Law of Attraction: 99 Teachings of Jesus, the Apostles, and the Prophets
The Book of Kelle: An Introduction to Goddess-Worship and the Great Celtic Mother-Goddess Kelle, Original
    Blessed Lady of Ireland
The Goddess Dictionary of Words and Phrases: Introducing a New Core Vocabulary for the Women's
    Spirituality Movement

WOMEN
Aphrodite's Trade: The Hidden History of Prostitution Unveiled
Princess Diana: Modern Day Moon-Goddess - A Psychoanalytical and Mythological Look at Diana Spencer's
    Life, Marriage, and Death (with Dr. Jane Goldberg)
Women in Gray: A Tribute to the Ladies Who Supported the Southern Confederacy

REPRINTS
A Short History of the Confederate States of America (author Jefferson Davis; editor Lochlainn Seabrook)

*Lochlainn Seabrook does not author books for fame and fortune,
but for the love of writing and sharing his knowledge.*

⋄⋇☙ **SeaRavenPress.com** ☙⋇⋄

Warning: SEA RAVEN PRESS BOOKS WILL EXPAND YOUR ★ MIND!

Christ Is All And In All

Rediscovering Your Divine Nature
And The Kingdom Within

Lochlainn Seabrook

JEFFERSON DAVIS HISTORICAL GOLD MEDAL WINNER

FOREWORD BY DR. JEREMY LOPEZ

Diligently Researched for the Elucidation of the Reader

2014
SEA RAVEN PRESS, NASHVILLE, TENNESSEE, USA

CHRIST IS ALL AND IN ALL

Published by
Sea Raven Press, Cassidy Ravensdale, President
PO Box 1484, Spring Hill, Tennessee 37174-1484 USA
SeaRavenPress.com • searavenpress@gmail.com

SEA RAVEN PRESS
SPIRITUAL BOOKS, REAL HISTORY!

1ˢᵗ SRP paperback edition, 1ˢᵗ printing, March 2014 • ISBN: 978-0-9913779-0-9
1ˢᵗ SRP hardcover edition, 1ˢᵗ printing, October 2020 • ISBN: 978-1-943737-90-1

ISBN: 978-0-9913779-0-9 (paperback)
Library of Congress Catalog Number: 2014933681

Christ Is All and In All: Rediscovering Your Divine Nature and the Kingdom Within, by Lochlainn Seabrook. Foreword by Dr. Jeremy Lopez. Includes endnotes, index, and bibliographical references. Portions of this book have been adapted from the author's other works.

Front/back cover design, photography, art, book design, layout, interior art by Lochlainn Seabrook
All images, graphic design, graphic art, and illustrations copyright © Lochlainn Seabrook
All images selected, placed, manipulated, and/or created by Lochlainn Seabrook ©
Cover image: "Christ's Entry Into Jerusalem," Lippo Memmi, 14ᵗʰ Century

✆ All are thrice spirit-blessed who read this little book. ✆

PRINTED & MANUFACTURED IN OCCUPIED TENNESSEE, FORMER CONFEDERATE STATES OF AMERICA

SEA RAVEN PRESS

Dedication

To the enlightened Saint Paul of Tarsus, who boldly and openly taught the theosistic doctrine of Man's Divine Nature: the Indwelling Christ.

Epigraph

Put on the new man, which is renewed in knowledge after the image of him that created him: Where there is neither Greek nor Jew, circumcision nor uncircumcision, Barbarian, Scythian, bond nor free: but Christ is all, and in all.

SAINT PAUL, COLOSSIANS 3:11

Contents

The Indwelling Christ knocking on the door of human consciousness.

Notes to the Reader

☦ All canonical Bible passages are from the King James Version (KJV), unless otherwise noted. As a result, my readings and interpretations will differ from those found in other versions. Because of this, I highly recommend the use of the KJV in combination with *Christ Is All and In All*.

☦ While I have retained the original text of the KJV, I have divided long Bible passages into paragraphs suited to modern readers (these often differ from the standard biblical divisions).

☦ Though many of the Bible's books are pseudepigraphical (that is, their authors are unknown or, more often, are falsely attributed), for simplicity's sake I use the authors ascribed by Christian tradition.

☦ All italics within quotes are mine.

☦ Bracketed words within quotes contain my comments and corrections.

☦ Though I am a Christian and this is a Christian book, it is not associated with any specific Christian denomination, sect, faction, church, society, schism, community, or cult. What it *is* associated with are the original and authentic teachings of Jesus as they appear in the New Testament.

Many if not most of these teachings derive from The Gospel of Q (from the German word *quelle*, "source"), a now lost document (though mentioned by 2nd-Century Bishop Papias of Hierapolis,[1] and also Paul)[2] containing the shared earliest oral traditions surrounding Jesus' sayings—which were liberally used by Matthew and Luke, and to some extent Mark, before it finally disappeared.[3] Thus, the Synoptic Gospels contain precious remnants of the Lord's actual thoughts and words, as I chronicle in my book, *Jesus and the Gospel of Q: Christ's Pre-Christian Sayings As Recorded in the New Testament*.

Paleographic evidence shows, of course, that the Gospel of Q predates the four canonical Gospels, with the earliest "layer" (known as Q1) probably being recorded as early as the 30s (shortly after Jesus' death), Q2 being composed sometime in the 40s and 50s, and Q3 written as late as the year 75.

The Q1 layer, part of the true and original Gospel of Jesus, does not mention or delve into His life, birth, baptism, messiahship, the Last Supper, His trial, crucifixion, transfiguration, resurrection, or ascension. Its earliest stratum also contains no apocalyptic warnings, no martyrological dogma, no complex theodicies, no salvific creeds, no named apostles, and no rules or instructions on how to organize and maintain the community of Q (which authored Q)—or any future type of "church" for that matter. Rather, as one would expect from the earliest followers of the Master (who were not "Christians" and never thought of themselves as such), Q centers not on Jesus, but on Jesus' *teachings*, one of the most important which included His life-altering doctrines on Theosis, or God in Man, the focus of this book.

Other Jesuine teachings from the Gospel of Q that are found in the New Testament are the Lord's Prayer, the Golden Rule, the Law of Attraction, the Beatitudes, and many of His parables, such as those concerning the all-important Kingdom of God, or what I term "the Realm of Divine Mind."

For those who are interested, other important sources for Jesus' original and authentic teachings are The Secret Gospel of Mark and especially The Gospel of Thomas (which could itself be a version of the Gospel of Q)[4]—the latter being another "sayings gospel," some of whose mantic doctrines can be found in the writings of early Christian mystics.[5]

✝ While this is largely a Christian work, individuals from any faith, or no faith, can benefit from reading it. This is because there is only One Source behind the entire Universe, whatever name we choose to give it: God, Christ, Chrishna, Buddha, Zeus, Hera, Jupiter, Juno, Yahweh, Ashtoreth, Jehovah, Asherah, Ra, Isis, Tammuz, Ishtar, Daghda, Danu, Brahma, Saraswati, Odin, Frigga, Nature, the Unified Field, or the Laws of Physics. How can this be? It is quite Simple. God manifests in your life according to how you perceive Him/Her/It, for the One is no respecter of persons.[6]

✝ The doctrines in this book will rarely be understandable to biblicists or to the rational book-educated mind. To borrow the words of Saint John Chrysostom, they will be revealed to the reader, "not by cleverness, but by the Holy Ghost, as we are able to receive it." (Jesus spoke similarly about his more mystical teachings.)[7]

✝ Bless the world by sharing the doctrines in *Christ Is All and In All* with your family members, friends, neighbors, and coworkers who want to hear the Word of God. Being eternal, the Word is still very much alive, and is ready to work miracles in the lives of all those who are prepared to receive it.[8]

Foreword

There has been a lot of talk over the years on the subject of the Christ and His position in the cosmos. During my own ministry I have discovered many spiritual principles, from learning to "live in the now moment" to the truth of the Universal Christ. I am not alone. There is a change taking place in the hearts and minds of people globally to reimagine, restructure, and reevaluate the way we have viewed the universe, creation, and God.

In his latest book, *Christ Is All and In All*, Lochlainn Seabrook has presented biblical truths that prompt us to completely rethink what we have been taught. It is indeed time to take a deeper look to see if God is boxed inside a four wall community, or, if He is bigger than what we have ever known.

In bringing out what it means to be created in God's image, Lochlainn answers the age old questions: Are we or are we not equal to God? Is He really God of all or merely God of some?

Many people today are daring to "walk on the water of secrets and mysteries" in order to find those deeper truths that set people free. Lochlainn is one of these: a "water walker" of deeper truths. This book will shift the paradigm from the limited Christ of institutionalized belief to the unlimited Christ of Spirit.

Organized religion for so long has kept us in the darkness of ignorance. But today we are starting to become enlightened with the light and life of the Christ Conscious mind, enabling us to see the divine nature that lives within each one of us. Instead of viewing Him as being part of a specific faith or denomination, we are now rising to the occasion to see the Universal Christ everywhere: Out of the ashes of human limitations into the unlimited cosmos of all things.

Lochlainn Seabrook's new book is a masterpiece! *Christ is All and In All* is full of God's glorious work, an invaluable gift to the world.

Dr. Jeremy Lopez
Author of *The Power of the Eternal Now*
drjeremylopez.com

The Father, the Son, and the Holy Ghost are ancient Pagan code names (later adopted by Christianity) for the One Life Force and Source of All, the Higher Self or Individual Soul, and the Activating Spirit or "Breath of God" respectively. Since this trinity is one, and since you are perfectly made in God's image, you possess all three of these within you, just as Paul said. Hence, Jesus declared "ye are gods," accorded all of the same powers and abilities He had. Your recognition and understanding of this reality ("self-realization") is your salvation, bestowing upon you "life everlasting," a truly marvelous promise given to us by every great spiritual teacher dating back to the dawn of history.

Introduction

THIS BOOK IS AN ANSWER to the many Christians who have asked me about our Divine Nature, wanting to know more. It is also fulfills a need for those who have never heard about our Indwelling Christ, and who are seeking answers.

There is a third group for whom I wrote this book: those Christians who John complained cannot comprehend the all-inclusive "light that shineth in the darkness";[9] that is, those who maintain that there is no such thing as our Inner Divinity, and who claim that the only "Christ" was the one crucified on Mount Calvary 2,000 years ago. These are the same individuals, we will note, who believe that we are frail mortal creatures who must strive for perfection in order to attain the Kingdom of God *after* we die.

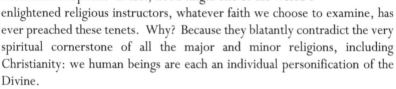

Anyone who has read their Bible closely will know, however, that these ideas are in complete opposition to what Jesus Himself taught, as well as the Apostles and the Old Testament Prophets. In fact, not a single one of the world's enlightened religious instructors, whatever faith we choose to examine, has ever preached these tenets. Why? Because they blatantly contradict the very spiritual cornerstone of all the major and minor religions, including Christianity: we human beings are each an individual personification of the Divine.

In this book we will explore the many biblical evidences of what is known as Theosis or Theosisism: the doctrine of our Inner Divinity, that is, God in Man. We will also examine how we came to have a Divine Nature, who gave it to us, why it was given to us, and what Paul meant when he said that you will "be risen with Christ . . . by his Spirit that dwelleth in you."[10]

The canon of Theosis, or Divine Immanence, as it is also known, was one of the main creeds of Jesus' arcanum, just one in a large body of what the Apostle Thomas called His "secret sayings,"[11] and what Jesus referred to as "The Gospel of the Kingdom [of God]."[12]

That this principle is no longer taught in our churches is not surprising: for political purposes the Lord's personal Gospel was long ago tossed aside (obliterated would be a more accurate word), ruthlessly replaced by the Ecclesia's manmade gospel called "The Gospel of Jesus Christ." In this way the focus went from the message to the messenger, from Jesus' Gospel about the Universal Christ to a Church-created dogma about Jesus Christ.[13]

In 1871 the great American Freemason and Confederate General Albert Pike wrote of this spiritual atrocity:

After the internal and Divine Word originally communicated by God to man, had become obscured; after man's connection with his Creator had been broken, even outward language necessarily fell into disorder and confusion. The simple and Divine Truth was overlaid with various and sensual fictions, buried under illusive symbols, and at last perverted into horrible phantoms. For in the progress of idolatry it needs came to pass, that what was originally revered as the symbol of a higher principle, became gradually confounded or identified with the object itself, and was worshipped; until this error led to a more degraded form of idolatry.[14]

This "degraded" Christian "idolatry" of Jesus occurred, of course, only after He died, for our egoless Lord would never have condoned the blind worship of Him that followed. Harken to the words of the One who consistently tried to discourage those who would form a cult in His name:

> *I can of mine own self do nothing*: as I hear, I judge: and my judgment is just; because *I seek not mine own will*, but the will of the Father which hath sent me. *If I bear witness of myself, my witness is not true.* . . . [Thus] *he that believeth on me, believeth not on me, but on him that sent me.*[15] . . . [For] *the word which ye hear [me preach] is not mine*, but the Father's which sent me.[16]

Jesus' focus was always on God the Father, with whom, as with both Jesus[17] and the Holy Spirit,[18] we are one.[19] As the Master taught, this makes us "gods,"[20] earthly divinities that were "created in His image,"[21] a mystical relationship that Paul personally referred to as "the Son in me."[22]

With the suppression of His "secret sayings," the Gospel of the Kingdom—the true, original, and actual "Good News" of the Bible—Jesus' teachings on Theosis were largely lost as well, much to the detriment of the Christian laity and the clergy. This little book will help bring back and preserve the forgotten, misinterpreted, and concealed teachings of THE CHRIST who, thanks be to God, "is all and in all."[23]

Lochlainn Seabrook
God-written, Vernal Equinox, 2014
Nashville, Tennessee, USA
In Nobis Regnat Christus ("Within Us Reigns Christ")

Christ

Is All And In All

Rediscovering Your Divine Nature
And the Kingdom Within

"Those who decipher the inner meaning of my words will have eternal life."[24]

JESUS, The Gospel of Thomas

Although this early illustration is called "The Holy Trinity," it actually depicts one of the great secret teachings of Jesus, namely the doctrine of Theosis: God in Man. In His typically mystical but succinct manner, our Lord encapsulated the entire principle in a single beautiful passage: "*I am in my Father, and ye in me, and I in you.*"

1

Your Divine Nature

Part 1

WHO ARE YOU?

DO YOU KNOW WHO AND what you *really* are? All of the world's major religions, including Christianity, teach that we are made up of three basic parts: a body (our physical vehicle), a mind (our ego), and a soul (our spirit).[25] As a Christian you know that some part of yourself survives so-called "death." Since the body and the ego are left behind when we "die," you cannot be either of these.

So what are you? There is only one possibility.

You are your soul, or more to the point, you are a soul; a spiritual being who comes to earth and is temporarily encased in a material body that carries you about, and which includes an ego to help ensure your physical survival.

Due to the veil of amnesia that is purposefully drawn over us when we leave Heaven and enter the body, we forget what our true nature is, however. In turn, we tend to become attached to our bodies and egos during our short term here in Earth School, often mistaking them for the real "us." But we can only be a soul, and that is exactly what the Bible says we are:

> And the Lord God formed man of the dust of the ground, and breathed into his nostrils the breath of life; *and man became a living soul.*[26]

We are all at least dimly aware of what a soul is. Webster defines it as "the animating principle, or actuating cause of an individual life; the spiritual principle embodied in human beings." In other words, our soul, though a nonphysical form, is the unborn and undying inner structure of who we are, for our true nature is nonphysical.[27] This fact has been known for millennia. According to the ancient historian Josephus, for instance, nearly 2,000 years ago Eleazar ben Yair, the Jewish leader at the siege of Masada, had this to say about our spiritual essence:

> [The] soul . . . hath one nature, and that an incorruptible one also; but yet is it the cause of the change that is made in the body; for whatsoever it be which the soul touches, that lives and flourishes, and from whatsoever it is removed, that withers away and dies; such a degree is there in it of immortality.[28]

Our modern day pastors, ministers, and preachers have at least taught us this much. But what they often leave out is what our soul *actually* is; where it comes from, what it is made of, and what its capabilities are. This is unfortunate, for this knowledge is vital to learning how to create the earthly existence that Jesus planned for us: a life of happiness, health, and abundance!

ESTABLISHING OUR TRUE NATURE
The Bible is very clear on what our genuine nature is, how it came to be, what it can do, and why it was created to begin with. But before we consult the Good Book on these questions, in plain English let us lay out the basic facts of "who," "how," "what," and "why":

Who: God created us, our souls, as exact copies of Himself.
How: God created our souls using His divine powers.
What: As pieces of or copies of God our true nature is divine, and therefore imperishable: birthless, deathless, and ageless.
Why: We were given the godlike gift of divine immortality, and the unlimited powers that go with it, in order to experience the many joys of earthly life at optimum level.

Some of you, especially those who are unfamiliar with the Bible, may be thinking that while these are interesting statements, they are merely my opinions, for you have never heard them mentioned in church.

Actually, these are not opinions, mine or anyone else's, and they are indeed taken directly from the Bible. Now let us see where.

WHAT IT MEANS TO BE CREATED "IN GOD'S IMAGE"

The book of Genesis could not be more explicit on *who* created us and *how* we were created:

> And God said, "Let us make man in our image, after our likeness: and let them have dominion over the fish of the sea, and over the fowl of the air, and over the cattle, and over all the earth, and over every creeping thing that creepeth upon the earth." So *God created man in his own image*, in the image of God created he him; *male and female created he them.*[29]

There can be no confusion here: the Bible tells us that God created us "in His image," for, as the Freemasons say, "the essence of the Human Soul is the image of God."[30] And what is an image? Webster says it is an "exact reproduction, an exact likeness of the form of a person or thing." This means that we are not an imitation, a mere similitude or representation of God. We are an actual piece of God, what the ancients called a "divine spark" of the Supreme Being. Since God is divine, we are as well, just as Meister Eckhart declared: "The spark is so akin to God that it is one with God, and not merely united to Him."[31]

JESUS CALLED US "GODS"!

What does this mean exactly? It means that we are each a god or goddess in our own right. This is not my teaching. It is Jesus' teaching! Here from the Gospel of John are the Master's own words in answer to a question he was asked: *what* are we?

> Jesus answered them, is it not written in your law, 'I [God] said, "*Ye are gods?*"'[32]

And *why* were we created as divine beings? So that "our joy may be full," He stated.[33] We are meant to live a life of happiness, filled with laughter, wonderful experiences, and abundance in all areas, and as we will see, our Divine Nature allows us to do just that! Here is how the Freemasons describe the purpose of involution, the godly act of enfolding the soul in a physical body:

> [We teach] that the soul of man is formed by Him for a purpose; that, built up in its proportions, and fashioned in every part, by infinite skill, an emanation from His spirit, its nature, necessity, and design is virtue. It is so formed, so moulded, so fashioned, so exactly balanced, so exquisitely proportioned in every part, that sin introduced into it is misery; that vicious thoughts fall upon it like drops of poison; and guilty desires, breathing on its delicate fibres, make plague-spots there, deadly as those of pestilence upon the body. It is made for virtue, and not for vice; for purity, as its end, rest, and happiness.[34]

Finally, what is our innate divinity capable of? Does it really give us limitless powers? Jesus said "yes"!

> Verily, verily, I say unto you, *he that believeth on me, the works that I do shall he do also; and greater works than these shall he do.*[35]

We will have much more to say about this stunning fact. How sad that it is no longer a part of mainstream Christian doctrine!

Fortunately, it remains very much alive in Hinduism. Here is how the great Indian Savior Chrishna described the soul in the Bhagavad Gita:

> I myself never was non-existent, nor thou, nor these princes of the Earth; nor shall we ever hereafter cease to be. The soul is not a thing of which a man may say, "it hath been," or "is about to be," or "is to be hereafter"; for it is a thing without birth; it is pre-existent, changeless, eternal, and is not to be destroyed with this mortal frame.[36]

THE SOURCE OF JESUS' TEACHING ON OUR DIVINITY

You have seen the biblical evidence: God says that He made us as precise replicas of Himself, while Jesus declares that we are "gods." But where did our Savior get this notion, that we are deities, divinities with the power to perform not only the same miracles He did, but supernatural works even greater?

A close reading of the above scripture reveals the answer. Jesus says: "Is it not written in your law, 'I said, "Ye are gods?"'" The "law" He is referring to is the Law of Moses, the ancient Hebrew doctrines found in the first five books of what Christians view as part of the Old Testament, and which Jews call the Torah.

Thus, the idea that each one of us is a god is not original to Jesus. It was known to countless ancient biblical prophets, philosophers, adepts, and writers who lived centuries even millennia before Jesus. Let us look at some of these early passages.

In the book of Genesis, according to Moses, it is written:

> And the Lord God said, "Behold, the man [Adam] is become as one of us . . ."[37]

This concept is found in other Old Testament books as well, such as Psalms, the book that Jesus cites in the Gospel of John:

> I have said, "Ye are gods; and all of you are children of the most High."[38]

Here is how this doctrine appears in the book of Isaiah:

> Shew the things that are to come hereafter, that we may know that ye are gods . . .[39]

A UNIVERSAL PRE-BIBLICAL CONCEPT

According to Western religious tradition, Genesis was written nearly 3,400 years ago, or around 1400 B.C.; Psalms (actually a collection of poems) was written between 3,200 and 2,500 years ago, or between 1,200 and 500 B.C.; and Isaiah was written about 2,700 years ago, or around 700 B.C.

These ancient Hebrew concepts derive from even older religions and philosophies, many dating back to the very dawn of recorded history some 8,000 years ago, and even beyond into the prehistoric era.

It is clear then that the idea that we have a Divine Nature has been an integral part of human spirituality from the very beginning of our existence, extending all the way up through nearly every known society and religion, from ancient Egypt to modern America; from Hinduism, Wicca, Judaism, and Buddhism, to Zoroastrianism, Jainism, Druidry, and Christianity.[40]

JESUS DIED TO TEACH US THE DIVINE DOCTRINE OF THEOSIS

Despite its noble and ancient history, the idea that we are each deities in our own right greatly angered people in Jesus' day. And it is still upsetting people 2,000 years later. Indeed, it was this very doctrine that caused some, even among Jesus' friends, to say that He was possessed by a demon, and that He was insane.[41] And, according to the New Testament, it was this same "blasphemous" teaching that caused the Jews to rise up in anger against Him, and which ultimately led to His crucifixion.[42]

As we are about to see, however, this prejudice against Jesus was truly unwarranted, for not only does the Old Testament substantiate this particular teaching, but so do the words, beliefs, and writings of the early Church Fathers as well.

EXPOSING MAINSTREAM SCRIPTURE TWISTING

Amazingly, despite the bold proclamations from God and Jesus (the ultimate spiritual authorities) that we are divine, there are some in the formalistic Christian community who maintain that the Master did not mean what He said when He asserted that you and me are deities.[43] Because they do not believe in or cannot bring themselves to believe in our Inner Divinity, they maintain that He was using the word "gods" (in the Bible from the Greek word *theos*) to mean "human rulers," such as magistrates or judges.

Let us look at this more closely for a moment by examining the entire scriptural scene as recorded in the King James Version. I have included the word *theos* to show where it is used in the original Greek text:

> And it was at Jerusalem the feast of the dedication, and it was winter. And Jesus walked in the temple in Solomon's porch.
>
> Then came the Jews round about him, and said unto him, "How long dost thou make us to doubt? If thou be the Christ, tell us plainly." Jesus answered them, "I told you, and ye believed not: the works that I do in my Father's name, they bear witness of me. But ye believe not, because ye are not of my sheep, as I said unto you. My sheep hear my voice, and I know them, and they follow me: and I give unto them eternal life; and they shall never perish, neither shall any man pluck them out of my hand. My Father, which gave them me, is greater than all; and no man is able to pluck them out of my Father's hand. *I and my Father are one.*"
>
> Then the Jews took up stones again to stone him. Jesus answered them, "Many good works have I shewed you from my Father; for which of those works do ye stone me?" The Jews answered him, saying, "*For a good work we*

stone thee not; but for blasphemy; and because that thou, being a man, makest thyself God [theos]." Jesus answered them, "Is it not written in your law, 'I said, Ye are gods [theos]?' If he called them gods [theos], unto whom the word of God [theos] came, and the scripture cannot be broken; Say ye of him, whom the Father hath sanctified, and sent into the world, 'Thou blasphemest'; because I said, 'I am the Son of God [theos]'? If I do not the works of my Father, believe me not. But if I do, though ye believe not me, believe the works: that ye may know, and believe, that the Father is in me, and I in him."

Therefore they sought again to take him: but he escaped out of their hand, and went away again beyond Jordan into the place where John at first baptized; and there he abode. [44]

Obviously, if Jesus was using the word "gods" to mean "human rulers," His statements here become utterly nonsensical, for the simple fact that *if one calls himself a "human ruler," it is not blasphemy.* The Pharisees would have only considered Jesus' statement blasphemous if He had used the word "gods" to mean "deities," that is, divine beings. It is self-evident then that this is exactly what He meant, for He repeated this same doctrine, in various forms, over and over throughout His earthly ministry. [45]

"I IN THEM"
Let us look, for example, at a part of the prayer Jesus uttered following the Last Supper. As He clearly states, His petition concerns not just the Twelve Apostles, but *all* believers:

Neither pray I for these alone, but for them also which shall believe on me through their word; *That they all may be one; as thou, Father, art in me, and I in thee, that they also may be one in us:* that the world may believe that thou hast sent me. *And the glory [powers] which thou gavest me I have given them; that they may be one, even as we are one: I in them, and thou in me, that they may be made perfect in one;* and that the world may know that thou hast sent me, and hast loved them, as thou hast loved me. . . [46]

Plainly, Jesus is asserting that He and the Father are one, that we in turn are one with He and the Father, and that He has given us the same "glory," "perfection," and "love" that the Father has given Him. Though He uses typically mystical terminology here, our Lord has provided us with the consummate definition of the doctrine of Theosis: the Father, the Son, and humanity are all "made perfect in one"!

Jesus is portrayed here literally as the "Grand Archbishop of the Church." But our Lord did not found the religion that would later take its name from Him, for this event occurred long after His "death." So we must look to a mystical interpretation to understand this illustration, and it is this: THE CHRIST is universal and immortal, dwelling within all men and women as their Real Selves. And each individual is him- or herself a "Church" over which the Indwelling Christ is "Archbishop." As such He wears the "Crown of Life," for He truly is King over the Inner Realm of the Father, as Jesus Himself declared: "*Behold, the Kingdom of God is within you.*"

"CHRIST IS ALL AND IN ALL"

From Jesus the principle of Theosisism, that is, Man's Divine Nature, was passed onto His followers. Paul, more than any other Apostle, was keenly aware of our divinity, calling each one of us "an heir of God through Christ,"[47] after which he says: "Christ [will] be formed" *within* all believers.[48] To the Jesus community at Colossae Paul wrote the following remarkable passage, declaring that "Christ is in all":

> And [we] have put on the new man [attained a new level of consciousness by defeating our "old man," that is, the Lower Self], which is renewed in knowledge [Gnosis] after the image of him [God] that created him [Christ]: Where there is neither Greek nor Jew, circumcision or uncircumcision, Barbarian, Scythian, bond nor free: but *Christ is all, and in all*.[49]

The words in italics are so plain, so powerful, so breathtaking, that I have used them as the title for this very book!

Paul is obviously not speaking here of the religiopolitical title Christ ("anointed"), which—because they were considered divine—was given to all early Jewish kings and Pagan emperors,[50] and some lower ranked religious authorities as well.[51] Nor was he speaking of Mary's human son, "Jesus Christ."[52]

He is referring to "THE CHRIST,"[53] that is, the great Indwelling Christ,[54] or what he called the "Christ in you,"[55] the same Christ which he so revealingly says *"was also in Jesus."*[56] Let us note that Paul does not say that THE CHRIST "existed only in Jesus." He is clear: THE CHRIST "was *also* in Jesus," meaning that it is in us as well. John the Baptist was speaking of the Christ Within when he said, "there standeth one among you, whom ye know not."[57] Not physically "standing," but spiritually.

What is the significance of having THE CHRIST in us? Within you and me, operating as our Real Selves, we possess the likeness of the Divine, a true oneness with the Creator, which Paul refers to as being "equal with God."[58] And this is precisely what the first chapter of the first book of the Bible declares![59]

THE UNIVERSAL & IMMORTAL INDWELLING CHRIST

This is the same Christ that John referred to as *"the true Light which lighteth every man that cometh into the world,"*[60] for the Inner Christ is all-pervading, infinite, indestructible, limitless, and universal, *the only true reality*, just as Daniel noted:

> I saw in the night visions, and, behold, one like the Son of man came with the clouds of heaven, and came to the Ancient of days, and they brought him near before him. And there was given him dominion, and glory, and a kingdom, that all people, nations, and languages, should serve him: *his dominion is an everlasting dominion, which shall not pass away, and his kingdom that which shall not be destroyed.*[61]

Here is how the Hebraist phrased it: THE CHRIST, "who being the brightness of his glory, and the express image of his person, and *upholding all things by the word* of his power."[62]

Now if THE CHRIST (or Logos) is what has been animating "all things" from before the beginning of time, how could "He" have been born in only one man 2,000 years ago? According to Jesus Himself this idea is false. In fact, this orthodox Christian doctrine is a form of scripture-twisted biblical literalization that has only served to conceal the very Truth that our Lord came to reveal to humanity: Man is in God and God is in Man, and we are all one![63]

THE CHRIST WAS NOT BORN: HE HAS ALWAYS EXISTED

We should not be surprised to learn then that Jesus declared that what was known to the ancients as the preexistent "Lord of Lords, King of the Ages,"[64] or what we call THE CHRIST,[65] lived before He did. Here is how this sensational truth appears in the Gospel of Matthew:

> While the Pharisees were gathered together, Jesus asked them, saying, "What think ye of Christ? whose son is he?" They say unto him, "The Son of David." He saith unto them, "How then doth David in spirit call him Lord, saying, 'The Lord said unto my Lord, "Sit thou on my right hand, till I make thine enemies thy footstool?"' *If David then call him Lord, how is he his son?* And no man was able to answer him a word, neither durst any man from that day forth ask him any more questions.[66]

In the Gospel of John, Jesus—speaking as the ageless and immortal Universal Christ—says: "Verily, verily, I say unto you, Before Abraham was, I am."[67] In the book of Revelation Jesus describes the all-inclusive Christ this way: "I am Alpha and Omega, the beginning and the end, the first and the last."[68] That THE CHRIST existed prior to the world, even prior to the formation of the Universe, is clear from other statements made by the Master:

> What and if ye shall see the Son of man ascend up *where he was before?*[69]

> And now, O Father, glorify thou me with thine own self with the glory *which I had with thee before the world was.*[70]

> Father . . . thou lovedst me *before the foundation of the world.*[71]

CHRISTIANITY WAS NOT FOUNDED: IT HAS ALWAYS EXISTED

Our enlightened Lord—who was clearly a religionless Jewish mystic—did not found the organized Church that eventually took His name, for not only did He have no such a goal in mind,[72] authentic history shows that it was formed by His followers after His death.[73] Yet He well understood the eternal nature of both the Indwelling Christ and the Universal Spirituality (later called "Christianity") that He preached.

Indeed, if God's Truth, being "the same yesterday, and to day, and for ever,"[74] is immortal and unchanging, how then could Jesus have been the originator of it? Additionally, if THE CHRIST has always existed then true Christianity must have always existed as well, for one cannot "found" a religion that has no beginning and no end. This is why Voltaire said that Plato was "one of the greatest teachers of Christianity,"[75] and it is why Justin Martyr called Socrates "a Christian before Christ."[76] Yet, both Plato and Socrates were born four centuries *before* Jesus.

Like our Lord, these were Truth-realized men who understood that a timeless God indwells us, whatever name we choose to give Him!

Here is what the venerable Church Father Saint Augustine had to say on this subject:

> That which is known as the Christian religion existed among the ancients, and never did not exist; from the beginning of the human race until the time when Christ came in the flesh, at which time the true religion, *which already existed* began to be called Christianity.

Eusebius, the well-known ancient Roman Christian historian and the bishop of Caesarea in the early 4th Century, made a similar statement:

The names of Jesus and Christ were both known and honored by the ancients [that is, pre-Christian peoples]. . . . *That which is called the Christian religion is neither new nor strange, but*—if it be lawful to testify the truth—*was known to the ancients.*

Of the pre-Christian Jewish sect the Therapeutae, Eusebius writes:

. . . it is highly probable, that the ancient commentaries which he [Philo] says they have, are the very gospels and writings of the apostles . . .[77]

Early Gnostic Christians preached the identical doctrine. In their work entitled The Tripartite Tractate, we read:

Not only did the Christ exist from the very beginning [of time], *but so did the Church.*[78]

We have canonical evidence for these views as well. Paul, for example, acknowledged that the Indwelling Christ, and therefore Christianity, were both known to his own henotheistic ancestors, the Israelites, who, according to Jewish tradition, crossed the Red Sea some 1,500 years before the birth of Jesus:

Moreover, brethren, I would not that ye should be ignorant, how that all *our fathers* were under the cloud, and all passed through the sea; and were all baptized unto Moses in the cloud and in the sea; and did all eat the same spiritual meat; and did all drink the same spiritual drink: for *they drank of that spiritual Rock that followed them: and that Rock was Christ.*[79]

In his letter to the Ephesians Paul asserts that Jesus (the Indwelling Christ) chose us to be His "adopted children" even prior to the earth being formed:

According as he hath chosen us in him *before the foundation of the world*, that we should be holy and without blame before him in love: *having predestinated us* unto the adoption of children by Jesus Christ to himself, according to the good pleasure of his will . . .[80]

In his letter to the Colossians Paul makes this cosmic statement about the Indwelling Christ,

. . . who is the image of the invisible God, the firstborn of every creature: for by him were all things created, that are in heaven, and that are in earth, visible and invisible, whether they be thrones, or dominions, or principalities, or powers: *all things were created by him*, and for him: and *he is before all things*, and *by him all things consist.*[81]

The Apostle Peter wrote that THE CHRIST has always been recognized, but for the benefit of humanity was made known physically in the form of Jesus some 2,000 years ago:

Who verily was foreordained *before the foundation of the world*, but was manifest in these last times for you . . .[82]

As we have seen, the prophet Daniel, who lived some 600 years before the birth of our Lord, was also well aware of the World-Christ and His "everlasting" church, stating that "his dominion is *an everlasting dominion*, which shall not pass away, and his kingdom that which shall not be destroyed."[83]

And so it is clear from the words of the Church Fathers, Jesus, the Apostles, and the Prophets that THE CHRIST is boundless, timeless, and imperishable, and because as God He "formed *all* things,"[84] we are individual expressions of Him ourselves, just as the book of Genesis testifies.[85]

"PARTAKERS OF THE DIVINE NATURE"
In Peter's second letter we find this highly significant scripture concerning Theosis:

Whereby are given unto us exceeding great and precious promises: that by these *ye might be partakers of the divine nature.*[86]

The Hebraist said the same thing:

For they verily for a few days chastened us after their own pleasure; but he for our profit, that *we might be partakers of his holiness.*[87]

Webster defines the word partake this way: "to possess or share a certain nature or attribute." Thus, even though Bible literalists enjoy quibbling over the nuances of these two particular scriptures, to all thinking people their meaning is obvious: as human beings we each possess a Divine Nature, a share of the holy attributes of God Himself!

The Old Testament too brims with references to the immortal divinity that "is all, and in all."[88] In the book of Micah we find this esoteric description of the Imperishable Christ, which has existed from time immemorial:

> But thou, [town of] Bethlehem Ephratah, though thou be little among the thousands of Judah, yet out of thee shall he [THE CHRIST made manifest] come forth unto me that is to be ruler in Israel; *whose goings forth have been from of old, from everlasting.*[89]

THE SOLAR LIGHT OF THE INDWELLING CHRIST

King Solomon described our soul this way: "The spirit of man is the candle of the Lord."[90] This divine "candle" is the Christ Within, your Higher Self, which was totally realized and perfected in the self-actualized figure of our Lord Jesus, whose countenance, John said, was "as the sun,"[91] and whom Malachi foretold as the "Sun of Righteousness."[92]

The Sun being an archetypal symbol of both the Indwelling Christ and spiritual enlightenment (known in the East as the Atman and samadhi respectively),[93] Jesus was often portrayed in ancient Christian art as the Greek Pagan Sun-god Helios, soaring through the heavens in his fiery chariot.[94] And after Emperor Constantine merged Him with the Pagan Sun-god *Sol Invictus* ("Unconquerable Sun"),[95] Jesus' followers faced east each morning at dawn to worship Him under the Pagan god title *Sol Justitiae*, the "Sun of Justice."[96] Thus in the book of Revelation Jesus is equated with the astrological star sign Leo (the lion), which is ruled by the Sun,[97] while the Master Himself referred to THE CHRIST as "the light of the world."[98]

Mystically, the effulgent "sunlight" of Jesus is the light of THE CHRIST that exists within each one of us, within all things, in fact—which is why the 13th-Century Italian Saint Francis of Assisi referred to the Sun as "my Lord, Sir Brother Sun."[99] Jesus said: "Believe in the light, that ye may be the children of light,"[100] while Paul wrote: "Awake thou that sleepest, and arise from the dead, and Christ shall give thee light."[101] The inner meaning:

It is time to awaken from your spiritual torpor, and come up out of the coffin of dead religion. Allow the Indwelling Christ to enlighten your mind with the Truth.[102]

THE "CHRIST IN YOU, THE HOPE OF GLORY"

Here is another passage from Paul, this one from his letter to the Colossians, in which he refers to Jesus' message of Theosis as "the mystery which hath been hid from ages and from generations":

> I am made a minister, according to the dispensation [permission] of God which is given to me for you, to fulfil the word of God; even the mystery which hath been hid from ages and from generations, but now is made manifest to his saints: To whom God would make known what is the riches of the glory of *this mystery* among the Gentiles [nonbelievers]; which is *Christ in you*, the hope of glory.[103]

Here is the inner meaning:

> God has ordained me to spread a message, a secret that has been concealed from the ordinary from the beginning of time until now. The secret is this: Christ is not outside of you, *He is inside of you*. And because you are one with Christ, and because Christ is one with God, you too are one with God and therefore possess the glorious powers of God.[104]

Taken literally the following mystical Pauline scriptures are unintelligible. However, they make perfect sense if, as is absolutely true, we each possess the Universal World-Christ as our Soul-Selves:

> Therefore we are buried with him by baptism into death: that like as Christ was raised up from the dead by the glory of the Father, even so we also should walk in newness of life. For if we have been planted together in the likeness of his death, *we shall be also in the likeness of his resurrection*.[105] . . . But if the Spirit of him that raised up Jesus from the dead *dwell in you*, he that raised up Christ from the dead shall also quicken your mortal bodies by *his Spirit that dwelleth in you*.[106] . . . If *ye then be risen with Christ*, seek those things which are above, where Christ sitteth on the right hand of God. Set your affection on things above, not on things on the earth. For ye are dead, and *your life is hid with Christ in God*. When *Christ, who is our life*, shall appear, then *shall ye also appear with him in glory*.[107]

PAUL SAYS YOU ARE "EQUAL WITH GOD"!

Here is an amazing personal commandment from Paul to you and me:

> *Let this mind be in you, which was also in Christ Jesus*: who, being in the form of God, thought it not robbery *to be equal with God*.[108]

The inner meaning:

> *I want you to think just like Jesus did*: He realized that the Indwelling Christ, the Universal Divine Nature, the Higher Self, our True Self, is created in the image of God; thus *He did not think it wrong to see Himself as being equal with God*.[109]

It is not a crime to consider ourselves "to be equal with God." In fact, we are supposed to think exactly that! So saith the Thirteenth Apostle, who described THE CHRIST cosmically as "dwelling in the light which no man can approach unto; whom no man hath seen, nor can see."[110]

WE ARE ALL "SONS OF GOD"

As is obvious, biblical evidence for our Divine Nature is plentiful and widespread throughout the Bible. John tells us that we are made "sons of God"[111] merely from the enormous "love the Father hath bestowed upon us."[112]

What is a "son of God"? It is an ancient esoteric phrase referring to our intimate spiritual kinship with the Divine; in other words, the biblical "son of God" is a symbol of our Higher Self, our spiritual being (conversely the phrase "son of Man" refers to our Lower Self or material being).[113]

Just as your physical body is created in the image of your earthly parents, your spiritual body is created in the image of your divine parents, who are none other than the "us" or *Elohim* of the Old Testament (a word that is used 2,249 times in the Bible).[114] The common (mis)translation of the plural Hebrew word Elohim is the singular word "God," or sometimes "Jehovah" or "Yahweh."[115] Mystically, however, all four of these words are plural androgynic names that mean "the immortal Masculine and Feminine Principle."[116]

Paul says that anyone who is "led by the Spirit of God, they are the sons of God."[117] Are you led by God's Spirit? If so, you are a Son or

Daughter of God, divine inside and out!

Are you loved by God? Absolutely. For you are His child, made to perfection in His image.[118] Do you believe? Then you are a Son of God! Paul likened our "sonship" to "spiritual adoption":

> . . . we, when we were children, were in bondage under the elements of the world: but when the fulness of the time was come, God sent forth his Son, made of a woman, made under the law, to redeem them that were under the law, that we might receive the adoption of sons. And because ye are sons, God hath sent forth the Spirit of his Son into your hearts, crying, "Abba, Father." *Wherefore thou art no more a servant, but a son; and if a son, then an heir of God through Christ.*[119]

In The Acts of Paul and Thecla, Paul makes this comment:

> Blessed are those who follow the teachings of Jesus, for they shall be called *the sons of the Most High.*[120]

Jesus gives a lucid explanation of the "sons of God" concept in *The Aquarian Gospel of Jesus the Christ*:

> *When man comes to himself and comprehends the fact that he is son of God*, and knows that *in himself lies all the powers of God*, he is a master mind and all the elements will hear his voice and gladly do his will. Two sturdy asses bind the will of man; their names are Fear and Unbelief. When these are caught and turned aside, the will of man will know no bounds; then man has but to speak and it is done.[121]

The Gospel of John states unequivocally that whoever believes "on the name" of Jesus automatically becomes a "son of God," or a Christ:[122]

> But as many as received him, *to them gave he power to become the sons of God*, even to them that believe on his name.[123]

THE TRUE GOSPEL: "GOD IS IN US"

In "receiving Him" we are sanctified with the "oil of gladness" by the Father,[124] giving us, like Jesus, possession of the Indwelling Christ,[125] anointed into Christhood by God Himself,[126] who Paul rightly asserts "is all and in all."[127] And just as it was said about both Melchizedek and the Lord,[128] as a Son of God you are an eternal, unborn, deathless spirit, or "priest," as the ancients mystically termed it. Thus the Hebraist said:

> Without father, without mother, without descent, having neither beginning
> of days, nor end of life; but made like unto the Son of God; abideth a priest
> continually.[129]

No more perfect description of the World-Christ, the Universal
Indwelling Christ that lives within each one of us,[130] has ever been
uttered,[131] for THE CHRISTOS[132] is none other than Spiritual Law, Divine
Law, which was written in our "inward parts" (souls) before we were
born.[133]

Some 2,000 years ago Jesus' brother James wrote: "Blessed is the man that
endureth temptation: for when he is tried, he shall receive the crown of life,
which the Lord hath promised to them that love him." To "love him" means to
be Christlike, while the "Crown of Life" is an archetypal symbol of Theosis: God
in Man. Those who understand and embrace these two profound facts will be
symbolically crowned kings and queens, immortal godlike rulers over their own
Kingdom Within. Thus saith the Lord in John 10:34. If this be heresy, Jesus was
the world's greatest heresiarch.

Here we have part of Jesus' original Gospel, what He called "The
Gospel of the Kingdom,"[134] and what is actually the true "Good News."
And it was for this very reason that the Apostle John, the most spiritually
advanced of all the Master's students,[135] gave Christ Himself the mystical
title "The Everlasting Gospel,"[136] or in modern parlance, "The Ageless
Good-Tale."[137] And we are each a part of this "Living Gospel," for as
Paul said of our Divine Nature, "Man is the image and glory of God,"[138]
the "perfect man" who has come "unto the measure of the stature of the
fulness of Christ."[139]

We will remember, according to Genesis, that whether male or female we are exact duplicates of God the Great Androgyne,[140] for during the Creation of the Universe

> God said, "Let *us* make man in our image, after our likeness" . . . So *God created man in his own image, in the image of God created he him; male and female* created he them.[141]

This statement can only mean that Theosisism is not a Jewish or a Christian doctrine. It is a universal one, known among the enlightened of every society dating back to before recorded history. Thus, the pre-Christian Pagan Roman poet Ovid could say right along with Jesus, *Est deus in nobis*: "God is in us."[142]

Strangely, many Christians today continue to resist this obvious Gospel Truth, so manifestly taught by our Lord. Most assuredly, Ovid's Roman contemporary Seneca once said, "the time will come when our posterity will wonder at our ignorance of things so plain."

The Bible makes little sense if read literally. This is because its authors did not intend it to be interpreted literally. For example, mainstream Christianity tells us that the seven encircled doves in this illustration symbolize the "seven churches" in the book of Revelation, and so they do—in the literal sense. But is the sense in which they were actually meant to be understood? Ancient religious artists, as well as the writers of the Old and New Testaments, were adepts and mystics who hid important spiritual truths inside of symbols, figures, emblems, myths, allegories, fables, folk tales, numbers, geometry, apologues, fantasies, lore, and legends. The many statements of Jesus (John 2:19-21; Matthew 12:40), John (Revelation 11:8), and Paul (Galatians 4:24), among many others, all definitively corroborate this fact. So we can be sure that there is something much deeper going on here, and indeed there is. There are seven musical tones, seven colors in the rainbow, seven holes in the head, seven ancient planets, seven ancient Wonders of the World, seven weekdays, seven early civilizations, ad infinitum. But there is something more specifically significant for us: there are seven energy centers (known to Hindus as *chakras*, "wheels") in the human body, located along the spine (the "serpent" of the Garden of Eden story). As our spiritual consciousness evolves, it moves upward from the lowest chakra (located at the base of the spine) until it reaches the highest (located at the top of the head), the Crown Chakra, symbol of Christ Consciousness: the fully God-realized individual. The dove-wheels above now take on a new and profound meaning not available to biblicists. Jesus taught using parables for the same reason. When His disciples, His advanced initiates, asked Him why, He gave this cryptic reply: "Because it is given unto you to know the mysteries of the kingdom of heaven, but to them it is not given.... Therefore speak I to them in parables: because they seeing see not; and hearing they hear not, neither do they understand." In other words, parabolic (that is, symbolic) teaching, as Jesus engaged in, is meant to conceal esoteric wisdom from the "profane" who might misuse and abuse it, while making it accessible to the more spiritually mature, who will use it to improve their lives, as well as the world around them. Those who read the Bible literally, that is, using their five senses instead of their sixth sense, imperil themselves. But those who learn to read intuitively rather than rationally will reap many benefits, including gaining an understanding of "the mysteries of the kingdom of heaven." They can then say along with the great Christian mystic Paul: "God hath made us able ministers of the new testament; not of the letter, but of the spirit: for the letter killeth, but the spirit giveth life."

2

Your Divine Nature

Part 2

THE "SON IN YOU" PERFECTLY MIRRORS GOD

PAUL CONSISTENTLY SUSTAINED THE FACT of Theosis, avowing that we have all been "anointed," that is, christed,[143] and so now "the Truth of Christ is *in* us"[144]—for as with Paul we are all literally and personally born with the "Son *in* me."[145]

Conversely, we are also *in* THE CHRIST, as the Apostle John remarked in his first letter:

> He that believeth on the Son of God hath the witness *in* himself. . . .[146] And we know that the Son of God is come, and hath given us an understanding, that we may know him that is true, and *we are in him* that is true, even *in* his Son Jesus Christ. This is the true God, and eternal life.[147]

Furthermore, John declared, all believers "have an unction [christing] from the Holy One."[148] Now, since the "Christ is formed *in* you,"[149] He also dwells *in* you, and because "Christ is the image of God,"[150] we must have been sculpted in the same image—for we are exact representations of the Father,[151] whom ancient Gnostic Christians called "the Divine Majesty."[152] We perfectly reflect His glory then, or as Paul put it:

But *we all*, with open face beholding as in a glass the glory of the Lord, *are changed into the same image* from glory to glory, even as by the Spirit of the Lord. [153]

THE INDWELLING CHRIST IS THE REAL YOU

Since we are *all* exact copies of God, individuations of the Divine—like perfect reflections in a looking glass Paul says—we need not search outside ourselves for proof of God, as so many people mistakenly do. You yourself are totally infused with what the Hindu calls *prana* (God's invisible Life Force). This means that you are godly throughout every cell, for *THE CHRIST is you, your True Self!* [154] Hence Jesus said:

If any man shall say unto you, "Lo, here is Christ," or "there"; believe it not. [155]

If this still seems like a foreign concept to you, take heart. Even many of the Master's closest and most spiritually mature initiates could not grasp this fact. The following exchange took place, for example, between Jesus and His Apostles. As He so often did, Jesus is speaking here as the Universal Indwelling Christ [156] that exists within each one of us: [157]

Philip saith unto him, "Lord, shew us the Father, and it sufficeth us." Jesus saith unto him, "Have I been so long time with you, and yet hast thou not known me, Philip? *he that hath seen me hath seen the Father*; and how sayest thou then, 'Shew us the Father'? Believest thou not that *I am in the Father, and the Father in me? the words that I speak unto you I speak not of myself: but the Father that dwelleth in me, he doeth the works.* Believe me that *I am in the Father, and the Father in me*: or else believe me for the very works' sake." [158]

This is Jesus' typically mystical way of saying that we are one with God, the Divine Mind, which He referred to as the "Father." And the part of us that makes us one with Him is the Indwelling Christ, our Higher Self, our incorporeal True Self!

Indeed, our physical bodies—though they are like mud pots, jars of clay, [159] mere "earthen vessels"—are filled with a staggering spiritual "treasure": [160] the life energy of the Christ Within which is "made manifest in our mortal flesh." [161] This is why Jesus taught that we should not call anyone "master" (that is, teacher), and it is why Paul said that once you realize and accept your Divine Nature you will no longer need "a schoolmaster,"[162] that is, external teachers.[163]

You see, there is only one true teacher and that is the Indwelling Christ,[164] who will teach you anything you want to know,[165] passing this "self-revealed" knowledge (Gnosis) directly from His Spirit into yours.[166]

"JESUS CHRIST IS IN YOU"

The Psalmist tells us that we were made "a little lower than the gods," then crowned with divine "glory and honour."[167] Paul goes even further, saying that "we shall judge angels,"[168] while Jesus taught that those who realize their Divine Nature are "equal unto the angels."[169] Reverend Billy Graham describes angels as divine beings who act as God's personal agents, and who serve as spiritual guardians of humanity.[170]

In the book of Jeremiah, God gives Himself the title: "The Lord Our Righteousness."[171] What does this mean? God does not call Himself "The Lord *My* Righteousness." He uses the word "our," which refers to us, His children. This is a not so arcane allusion, of course, to our true nature, our Divine Nature,[172] which, as we have seen, Paul referred to as: "Christ *in* us, the hope of glory."[173] "Know ye not your own selves, how that Jesus Christ is *in* you?" he asked.[174]

Indeed, it is the universality of the Christ Within[175] that enables us to be "crucified"[176] and "raised up" alongside the resurrected Jesus.[177] If we did not possess the same Inner Christ as the Lord, this would not be possible. Think about that for a moment.

This is why Paul made this extraordinary comment, one you will seldom hear preached from the pulpit: "God revealed His son *in* me."[178] We are fellow human beings with Paul. If the "son" (THE CHRIST) is in him, then He is in us as well. Of course He is. For as we have seen, the Interior Christ is both universal[179] and immortal![180]

Is this blasphemy? Absolutely not. It is ordained scripture! And by ignoring it we thwart the dazzling divine plan that God has in store for us.

THE GREAT I AM

Arguably the most obvious biblical references to our personal Godhood are to be found in the book of Psalms and the book of Exodus. In the former the Father declares: "Be still, and know that *I am God*."[181] In the latter Moses asks God what His name is, and God gives this answer:

> *I AM THAT I AM* . . . Thus shalt thou say unto the children of Israel, *I AM* hath sent me unto you.[182]

The Divine "I AM" spoken of here is what the Old Testament writers call "Jehovah"[183] and what the New Testament writers call "THE CHRIST."[184] In other words, the Great I AM is your authentic inner nature, your Divine Nature;[185] it is the real you, your genuine self. Moses, a fully enlightened initiate of the Egyptian Mystery Schools, understood his oneness with the Father, for he used the phrase "I AM" to identify himself with God when He appeared to the prophet from inside a burning bush:

> And when the Lord saw that Moses turned aside to see, God called unto him out of the midst of the bush, and said, "Moses, Moses." And Moses said, "Here *I am.*"[186]

Paul too, another illumined graduate of the Sacred Mysteries, was well versed in the use of this divine mystical name, saying:

> But by the grace of God *I am what I am*[187] . . . [Thus] I beseech you, be as *I am*; for *I am* as ye are.[188]

The Great I AM is spelled *Aum* or *Om* in Hinduism, *Amam* in Hebrew, *Hum* in Tibetan, *Amon* in ancient Egyptian texts, and *Amen* in mainstream Christianity (all mean "faithful"), and it is represented by the creative *Logos* or *The Word* in Gnostic Christianity,[189] and as Sol-*Om*-On (Solomon) in Kabbalah.[190]

John the Apostle used the Great I AM cryptically in the Greek word "Om-ega" (Omega),[191] even employing it as a noun: "*The* Amen, the faithful and true witness, the beginning of the creation of God."[192] This is why Pliny referred to the I AM as *Artifex Omnium Natura*: the "Architect of the Universe."

The magnificent and immortal I AM is your essence. Though it is within you, it is the end all and be all of everything, the true Alpha and Omega[193]—for it is a piece of God Himself, and God is all.[194]

The I AM is that aspect of you that answers when someone asks you who are you are: "I am (your name)." It is that which stares back at you from behind your eyes when you look in a mirror, just as Paul testified.[195] Thus 5,000 years ago, Isis, the supreme Mother-Goddess of ancient Egypt, could say: "I AM what was and is and is to come."[196]

THE I AM IS YOUR HIGHER SELF

The I AM is not your Ego, your false self, your human self, your Lower Self—which will perish with your material body (for "all flesh is grass").[197] It is your eternal God-Nature, your lucent Divine Self, your immortal God-Self; the "Christ that is formed *in* us,"[198] that is "*in* all of us,"[199] as Paul put it. It is that spiritual part of you which God "created in his own image":[200] the *perfect* you! Thus Jesus said: "Be ye therefore perfect, even as your Father which is in heaven is perfect."[201]

The I AM, AMEN, AMON, AUM, or OM is your Higher Self, your Divine Self, the incorporeal Supreme Self, the mystics' Cosmic Man, the Hindus' "Atman," Paul's "inner man"[202] or "inward man,"[203] Peter's "hidden man of the heart,"[204] Luke's "Holy One,"[205] Daniel's "Ancient of Days."[206] It is that part of you that was never born and will never die, and which is "the same yesterday, and to day, and for ever."[207] For the Indwelling "Christ abideth for ever."[208]

The I AM is one more common term for the Immortal Indwelling Christ that lies at the core of us all,[209] and which Jesus, like other ancient spiritual teachers, often used to announce His divinity to others: "I AM he," he once told a group of startled Pharisees, who then "fell to the ground."[210]

Here is another revealing exchange He had with this rigidly religious Jewish sect:

> Again the high priest asked him, and said unto him, "Art thou *the Christ*, the Son of the Blessed?" And Jesus said, "*I am* . . ."[211]

Jesus used the mystical I AM title repeatedly. Here are some other examples:

"I AM from above."[212]
"I AM the bread of life."[213]
"I AM the door of the sheep."[214]

"I AM the good shepherd."[215]
"I AM the light of the world."[216]
"I AM he that liveth."[217]
"I AM Master and Lord."[218]
"I AM meek and lowly in heart."[219]
"I AM a king."[220]
"I AM the way, the truth, and the life."[221]
"I AM the true vine."[222]
"I AM THE CHRIST."[223]

In mystical Christianity the "I AM" the Master speaks of here is not Himself, His personal Ego. It is not the human being, the illumined teacher, prophet, and healer named Jesus, who was known by the first Christians as the mortal son of Joseph and Mary[224]—whom Paul rightly said "was made of the seed of David according to the flesh."[225] Nor is it the man Jesus who, according to original Luke, was imbued with the Holy Spirit (that is, enlightenment) at the moment of His baptism (symbolized by the dove descending upon Him as "the Spirit of God").[226]

Rather it is (as the last example from the above list reveals) "*THE* CHRIST" that dwells within, which being universal,[227] exists in each one of us as our Higher Self.[228] Thus in The Gospel of Thomas Jesus says:

> I AM the True Light that shines over all. I AM everything. From me all things were given life, and to me all things will return. Cut open a log and I AM there. Lift up a rock and there you will find me.[229]

Tragically, this doctrine, which is known in one form or another in every religion, is the same one that the Jews in Jesus' day called "blasphemy,"[230] and in Paul's day "heresy,"[231] and which many uninformed Christian authorities today still think of as an impious sacrilege. Being an expression of God, of the Divine Mind, the Indwelling Christ or the Great I AM is the power of creative thought incarnate in Man. It is "the Word [that is, thought] made flesh."[232] Thus the 17th-Century French philosopher René Descartes said: "I think, therefore I AM."

Jesus is depicted here as the "Creator," manifesting *nine* creations, using the most occultic and mysterious of all numbers: no matter how nine is multiplied or what numbers are added to it, the numerological total can always be reduced to nine (e.g., 9+8=17, 1+7=9; 9x125=1,125, 1+1+2+5=9). In Christian symbolism nine is an emblem of the Holy Trinity squared, the Triple-Goddess squared (Christianized as the "Three Marys," John 19:25), and the number of the nine months of human pregnancy, among other arcane matters. The Truth, however, is that Jesus did not "create" anything—as He Himself testified. The true Creator is Divine Mind, or what He called "the Father," and according to the secret teachings of Jesus, your soul, THE CHRIST, is one with Him, making you a personal cocreator with God. Of this spiritual copartnership Paul correctly said: "It is God which worketh in you," for "we are labourers together with Him" in the creation of our daily lives here in Earth School. Hence the words of Jesus, speaking as the "Son" or Indwelling Christ: "*Verily, verily, I say unto you, the Son can do nothing of himself. . . . Believest thou not that I am in the Father, and the Father in me? [for] the words that I speak unto you I speak not of myself: but the Father that dwelleth in me, he doeth the works. . . . [Thus] he that believeth on me, believeth not on me, but on him that sent me.*" You will never hear these "heretical" doctrines taught at church. But for those who are sincerely interested in their personal spiritual growth, they can still be found in the King James Bible, available for all to read, study, and ponder.

WE ARE ALL "ABRAHAMS"

Being unlimited, boundless, and ubiquitous, the Inner Christ must have existed prior to the birth of Jesus, and indeed it did, as He Himself admitted.[233] As we have seen, the Lord, in His usual mystical way, explained it like this: "Before Abraham was, I AM."[234]

The magnificent import of this statement can be seen in the occult fact that Abraham's birth name was Abram,[235] which means "exalted Father." The "Father" is the esoteric biblical term for the Divine Mind, the Great Cosmic Spirit, the Cosmic Intellect, or what the ancient Egyptians knew as "Father Mind" or "Supreme Mind." The Sanskrit word for this, the immanent and infinite "One Absolute Reality," is Brahman. Thus Abram was the ancient Hebrew version of the Hindu Brahman: "a Brahman," in fact, who was later renamed A-Brahman, that is, Abraham[236]—whose name means "Father of a multitude," the "multitude" being everything in the Universe.[237]

Here again, speaking as the Indwelling Christ, the Universal Higher Self, we have Jesus speaking to the Pharisees, who represent the human Ego, or on a broader scale, the Universal Lower Self:

> "Ye are from beneath; I am from above: ye are of this world; I am not of this world. I said therefore unto you, that ye shall die in your sins: for if ye believe not that I am he, ye shall die in your sins. . . . I have many things to say and to judge of you: but he that sent me is true; and I speak to the world those things which I have heard of him." They understood not that he spake to them of the Father. Then said Jesus unto them, "When ye have lifted up the Son of man, then shall ye know that I am he, and that I do nothing of myself; but as my Father hath taught me, I speak these things."[238]

The inner meaning:

> "You act out of your Lower Selves; I act out of my Higher Self; you are religious; I am spiritual; therefore I say that if you do not believe in the Universal I AM that I AM, you will suffer due to your disbelief." . . . The Pharisees did not understand that Jesus was talking about the Divine Mind, so He said to them: "When you honor the Son of Man, the human Jesus, you will realize that I AM that I AM; and that I do nothing for my own honor; but only those things that the Divine Mind has directed me to say and do."[239]

As He so often did, Jesus is telling us that the Universal Indwelling

Christ[240] is one with the Father ("I AM"),[241] that is, with Divine Mind;[242] for, as Paul taught, Christ possesses the full nature of God.[243]

Now if, as the Master asserted, "I and my Father are one,"[244] and we are one with Christ[245]—in fact, He is *in* us[246] and we are *in* Him[247]—then we humans are also one with the Father,[248] and can therefore be nothing less than gods and goddesses ourselves.[249] For Christ and the Father are one and the same, and we are one with both![250]

Many people like to quibble, fight, and even war over which religion is "true." This idea, of "the one true faith" or "the one true religion," is quite illogical, however, and here is why.

By definition there is only a single "One": one Source, one Substance, one Cosmos, one Fire, one Mind, one Jehovah, one Brahman, one Ra, one Jupiter, one Zeus, one God over all, whether we are Christian, Jewish, or Pagan[251]—and we are all one with it.[252] Therefore the name we bestow on this energy, the Supreme Being, is immaterial. We are all worshiping the same God, whatever moniker we decide to give Him/Her/It. Thus Malachi wrote:

> Have we not all *one father*? Hath not *one God* created us?[253]

Paul made the following singular comments:

> But to us *there is but one God*, the Father, of whom are all things, and *we in him*; and one Lord Jesus Christ, by whom are all things, and *we by him*.[254]

> *One God and Father of all, who is above all, and through all, and in you all*.[255]

Why is there only one ultimate Source, one God? For the same reason we have only one heart: it would be impossible to synchronize two hearts. The second would always be slightly out of alignment with the first, disrupting the entire system.[256]

And so it is with the God of our Universe, a word that derives from the Latin *uni*, meaning "one" or "single." The Father Himself said:

> *I am* the Lord: that is my name: and my glory will I not give to another, neither my praise to graven images.[257]

Yes, there can be only one, and that "one" is the "living God,"[258] who

has invisibly expressed Himself in us as the Indwelling Christ.[259] It is
this, the Christ Within, whom Paul described as

> *the image of the invisible God, the firstborn of every creature*: for by him were all
> things created, that are in heaven, and that are in earth, visible and invisible,
> whether they be thrones, or dominions, or principalities, or powers: *all things
> were created by him, and for him: and he is before all things, and by him all things
> consist.*[260]

Because we are one with the One, just as Zen Buddhism holds that
we are each a Buddha, Jesus taught that each one of us is *a Brahman*; that
is, we are each an "Abraham," whose real self is the immortal Christ that
has always existed and will always exist.[261]

Our Lord made numerous mystical comments regarding our oneness
with the Universal Indwelling Christ:

> For where two or three are gathered together in my name, there am I in the
> midst of them.[262]

> Lo, I am with you alway, even unto the end of the world.[263]

> Verily I say unto you, inasmuch as ye have done it unto one of the least of
> these my brethren, ye have done it unto me.[264]

THEOSISISM IS A WORLDWIDE DOCTRINE

Some mistakenly believe that this idea is peculiar to Christianity.
Actually, Theosisism is preached around the globe in every major faith.

For example, just as the Old Testament prophets said we are all
deities,[265] just as Jesus said we are all gods,[266] just as Paul said we are all
"sons of Gods,"[267] "one in Christ,"[268] and just as God Himself said that we
are all immortal supernatural beings,[269] the Hindus too teach that we are
all what they refer to as "avatars": sparks of divinity that have descended
from Heaven to incarnate into mortal bodies.[270] The pre-Christian
Christians known as the Gnostics, espoused the exact same doctrine,
teaching that we are rays of the Heavenly Light, the "Sun of
Righteousness,"[271] a spiritual beam of energy which they called simply
"THE CHRIST."

In his 1871 book *Morals and Dogma*, lionized Freemason and

Confederate officer Albert Pike wrote:

> *The Soul of Man is Immortal*; not the result of organization, nor an aggregate of modes of action of matter, nor a succession of phenomena and perceptions; but an Existence, one and identical, *a living spirit, a spark of the Great Central Light, that hath entered into and dwells in the body*; to be separated therefrom at death, and return to God who gave it: that doth not disperse or vanish at death, like breath or a smoke, nor can be annihilated; but still exists and possesses activity and intelligence, even *as it existed in God*, before it was enveloped in the body.[272]

WHY YOU ARE AN INDIVIDUATION OF GOD

Jesus once described Theosis this way: "He that hath seen me hath seen the Father."[273] The inner meaning: "He that has realized his union with the Indwelling Christ has realized his oneness with the Divine Mind."[274] Paul referred to this mystically as "winning Christ,"[275] while the Hebraist asserted that the spiritually mature will become "partakers of his holiness."[276] Now you will understand the true significance of this statement by God, the Divine Mind: "I AM holy."[277]

Now you can also say, along with the Psalmist, "I AM holy,"[278] for the real you is a piece of the Father, and He is truly *holy*; that is, *whole-ly* (one). This means that we too, not just Jesus, possess what is called a hypostatic nature, in which both our human and divine aspects are unified.[279] For like the Lord, in each of us "dwelleth all the fulness of the Godhead bodily," making us *complete in Him*."[280]

Yes, we are all one within, one with the Cosmos, and one with each other, for God Himself is one.[281] However, though being ageless, timeless, and boundless allowed Him to exist everywhere and in all things simultaneously, He could not know Himself; He could not experience physical life on a personal level. In order to do so, He had to individuate Himself as finite matter. This He did by creating earthly life, which means that each one of us is a thought of the Divine Mind, or in biblical terminology, a "child of God"[282] frolicking on what Hindus call "God's playground": material creation.

We are all an aspect of the immeasurable, inexhaustible, everlasting Father, who is expressing Himself through us, and who is experiencing life through us via our many physical and spiritual senses. *You* are, in other words, the infinite, imperishable, indivisible consciousness of God, the Great and Limitless I AM![283]

The Victorian English biologist Herbert Spencer described God and our relationship to Him this way:

> God is infinite intelligence, infinitely diversified through infinite time and infinite space, manifesting through an infinitude of ever-lasting individualities.

Thus Paul could say: "So we, being many, are one body in Christ."[284] Here is this same concept in the words of Jesus: "I am in my Father, and ye in me, and I in you."[285] Our Savior Himself is telling us that we are *in* THE CHRIST and that THE CHRIST is *in* us.

Has any spiritual doctrine ever been more beautifully, perfectly, and obviously worded? Has any Christological idea ever been more openly preached and wonderfully self-evident?

THE CHURCH FATHERS ON THEOSIS

Though many modern Christians as well as Church authorities reject Jesus' doctrine of Theosis—God's deification of humanity—*all* of the early Church Fathers, in particular the Eastern Fathers,[286] heartily embraced this, the Great Master Secret, imparted by our Lord some 2,000 years ago. This is, after all, why Clement of Alexandria referred to Jesus as "the Teacher of the Divine Mysteries and Secrets." In 1903 Charles Webster Leadbeater wrote:

> The idea that man is capable of attaining this perfection, or deification as it is often called in the writings of the Fathers, would probably be considered sacrilegious by many of our modern theological writers, yet it was clearly held by the early Fathers, and they knew its attainment to be a possibility. Professor [Adolf] Harnack remarks that "deification was the idea of salvation taught in the Mysteries"; and again "after Theophilus, Irenaeus, Hippolytus, and Origen, *the idea of deification is found in all the Fathers of the ancient church, and that in a primary position.* We have it in Athanasius, the Cappadocians, Apollinarius [Apollinaris], Ephraem Syrus, Epiphanius, and others, as also in Cyril, Sophronius, and later Greek and Russian theologians."[287]

HIPPOLYTUS, AUGUSTINE, & MACARIUS

Here, for instance, is what the famed 3rd-Century theologian Hippolytus of Rome had to say about it:

For *thou hast become God*: for whatever sufferings thou didst undergo while being a man, these He gave to thee, because thou wast of mortal mould, but whatever it is consistent with God to impart, these God has promised to bestow upon thee, because *thou hast been deified, and begotten unto immortality*. This constitutes the import of the proverb, "Know thyself"; that is, *discover God within thyself, for He has formed thee after His own image*. For with the knowledge of self is conjoined the being an object of God's knowledge, for *thou art called by the Deity Himself*.[288]

Likewise, the estimable 4th-Century theologian Saint Augustine wrote:

And *we indeed recognize in ourselves the image of God*, that is, of the supreme Trinity, an image which, though it be not equal to God, or rather, though it be very far removed from Him,—being neither co-eternal, nor, to say all in a word, consubstantial with Him,—is *yet nearer to Him in nature than any other of His works, and is destined to be yet restored, that it may bear a still closer resemblance. For we both are, and know that we are, and delight in our being, and our knowledge of it*.[289]

The well-known 4th-Century Church Father Saint Macarius taught that the doctrines of the Incarnation and Redemption include the literal birth of THE CHRIST *inside* each individual, a spiritual union between Man and the Logos by which we are redeemed from *within* by God's sanctifying grace.[290]

LACTANTIUS, METHODIUS, & MEISTER ECKHART

Lactantius, the 4th-Century Christian author (and advisor to the Pagan-Christian Emperor Constantine I), wrote that those who live moral lives become, in every respect, perfectly indistinguishable from God.[291] The 4th-Century Church Father Saint Methodius taught that "every believer must, through participation in Christ, be born a Christ,"[292] and the 14th-Century German theologian Meister Eckhart held that just

as fire turns all that it touches into itself, so *the birth of the Son of God in the soul turns us into God*, so that God no longer knows anything in us but His Son.[293]

This highly honored Christian scholar also gave us the following notable quote concerning the doctrine of God in Man:

The Father speaks the Word into the soul, and when the Son is born, every soul becomes a Mary.[294]

IRENAEUS, ATHANASIUS, & GREGORY OF NAZIANZUS

The man who selected the four Gospels for inclusion in the New Testament, esteemed Church Father Saint Irenaeus, phrased Theosis this way:

> The Word of God was made man, and He Who is the Son of God, Son of Man, *that man blended with God's Word, and receiving the adoption, might become the Son of God.* . . . God by the Law and the Prophets promised to make His Saving One visible to all flesh, that He might become Son of Man, to the end *that Man also might become Son of God.* . . . Him alone thou wilt follow, Who is the True and Strong Teacher, The Word of God, Jesus Christ our Lord: Who for His immense love's sake was made that which we are, *in order that He might perfect us to be what He is.* . . . Thus, the Lord having redeemed us with His own Blood, and given His soul for our souls, and His own Flesh for our Flesh, and pouring out the Spirit of the Father for *the union and communion of God and man*; both bringing down God unto man by the Spirit, and again *bringing in man unto God* by His Incarnation, and in might and in truth, by His coming, bestowing upon us incorruption, by our Communion with Him.[295]

Citing one of my favorite scriptures, 2 Peter 1:4, Saint Athanasius, the 4th-Century Bishop of Alexandria, said this about the divinization of human beings:

> He [Jesus] has become Man, *that He might deify us in Himself*, and He has been born of a woman, and begotten of a Virgin, in order to transfer to Himself our erring generation, and *that we may become henceforth a holy race, and "partakers of the Divine Nature,"* as blessed Peter wrote.[296]

And again:

> For *Christ was made man that we might be made God*; and he manifested himself a body that we might receive the idea of the Unseen Father; and he endured the insolence of men *that we might inherit immortality*.[297]

The celebrated 4th-Century Archbishop of Constantinople, Gregory of Nazianzus, explained Theosisism this way:

> For He [Jesus] whom you now treat with contempt was once above you. He who is now Man was once the Uncompounded. What He was He continued

to be; what He was not He took to Himself. In the beginning He was, uncaused; for what is the Cause of God? But afterwards for a cause He was born. And that cause was that you might be saved, who insult Him and despise His Godhead, because of this, that He took upon Him your denser nature, having converse with flesh by means of Mind. While *His inferior Nature, the Humanity, became God, because it was united to God,* and became One Person because the Higher Nature prevailed . . . *in order that I too might be made God so far as He is made Man.*

CLEMENT, GREGORY OF NYSSA, THEOPHILUS, & AQUINAS

Based on Jesus' teaching that we are gods,[298] the illustrious 2nd-Century theologian Clement of Alexandria left us various instructions on Divine Man, saying that if one truly knows himself, he also knows God, which makes him like God.[299] God's Word or Logos came to earth as Man so that Man may learn that he too can become God. In fact, whoever possesses the Inner Logos (THE CHRIST), is God, which is certainly God's will.[300] This is why, alluding to Jesus' world-shaking theosistic statement in John,[301] Clement wrote,

> humans are called by the appellation of gods, being *destined to sit on thrones with the other gods* that have been first put in their places by the Savior.[302]

Saint Gregory, the 4th-Century Bishop of Nyssa, made this extraordinary statement:

> This is the safest way to protect the good things you enjoy: realize how much your Creator has honored you above all other creatures. He did not make the heavens in His image, nor the moon, the sun, the beauty of the stars, nor anything else which surpasses all understanding. *You alone are a similitude of eternal beauty, a vessel of happiness, a mirror image of the True Light. And if you look at Him, you will become what He is, imitating Him who shines within you, whose glory is reflected in your purity. Nothing in all of creation can equal your grandeur.* All the heavens can fit in the palm of God's hand. . . . And though He is so great, *you can wholly embrace Him: He dwells within you. He pervades your entire being.*

Saint Theophilus, the 2nd-Century bishop of Antioch, believed that "man, by keeping the commandments of God, may receive from him immortality as a reward, and *become God.*"[303] In his massive work *Summa Theologica*, world renowned 13th-Century Italian saint and theologian

Thomas Aquinas made these fascinating comments:

> When it is said that "God was made Man," the making is taken to be terminated in the human nature. Hence, *properly speaking, this is true: "God was made Man."*[304]

> All living creatures belong to their own species, yet *each participates in some way or another in the reflection of the Divine Essence.*[305]

> Now men are called the children of God in so far as *they participate in the likeness of the only begotten and natural Son of God*, Who is Wisdom Begotten. Hence by participating in the gift of wisdom, *man attains the sonship of God.*[306]

PAUL & THE CHRISTIAN MYSTICS ON THEOSIS

The always mystical Paul had this to say about THE CHRIST, whom he refers to here as the "Son," the "firstborn" who indwells us all:

> And we know that all things work together for good to them that love God, to them who are the called according to his purpose. For whom he did foreknow, *he also did predestinate to be conformed to the image of his Son*, that he might be the firstborn among many brethren. Moreover whom he did predestinate, them he also called: and whom he called, them he also justified: and whom he justified, them *he also glorified.*[307]

Noted Christian mystics, some of the Church's greatest advocates of Theosis, or what they called the "Doctrine of Immanence," also had plenty to say about our innate Godhood. The 12th-Century Saint Hildegard of Bingen, for instance, believed that God is a divine luminance that vivifies not just Man, but all living creatures, from blue whales down to the tiniest microbes, while the 13th-Century Beguine Mechtild of Magdeburg too saw the Divine Spark in all things, even so-called "inanimate" objects, such as stones.[308]

In *The Divine Comedy*, 14th-Century Italian mystic and poet Dante Alighieri calls God "the One who moves *all* things," "the glory" who "penetrates through the universe."[309]   The 19th-Century Swiss philosopher and Christian mystic Henri-Frédéric Amiel agreed with Hinduism[310] in stating that realizing our Divine Nature should be our number one goal:

> *To become Divine is . . . the aim of life*: then only can truth be said to be ours beyond the possibility of loss, because it is no longer outside of us, nor even in us, but *we are it, and it is we*; we ourselves are a truth, a will, a work of God. Liberty has become nature; *the creature is one with its Creator*—one through love.[311]

In her *Revelations of Divine Love*, 14th-Century English Christian mystic Julian of Norwich wrote:

> For as the body is clad in clothe, and the flesh in skin, and the bones in flesh, and the heart in the bulk [whole], *so are we soul and body clad and enclosed in the goodness of God* . . . for all they vanish and waste away, [yet] the goodness of God is ever whole and more near to us without any comparison.[312]

GNOSTICS, TRANSCENDENTALISTS, HINDUS, & SUFIS
Our great Christian philosophers (that is, the Christian Gnostics) have said much the same thing, like Victorian Transcendentalist Ralph Waldo Emerson, who wrote:

> *Within man is the soul of the whole*, the wise silence, the universal beauty, to which every part and particle is *equally* related—*the Eternal one.*[313]

This is possible because, as Paul noted, God is the substance in which "we live, and move, and have our being."[314] In other words, the Divine is both immanent and transcendent: it is both within us and without us. Or as the Hindu teacher Paramahansa Yogananda once so perfectly phrased it, God is both the light bulb and the light emanating from it.[315]

Can Jesus, the Apostles, the Old Testament prophets, *all* of the Church Fathers, our mystical and philosophical brothers and sisters, even

God Himself, all be wrong about a spiritual doctrine that has existed since the beginning of historical records among all people, in all societies, in all religions, right up to and into modern times?

Sufism too teaches that the realization of one's Divine Nature is the supreme reason behind incarnating on earth, the very objective of humanity's search for truth, meaning, and purpose. Thus the great spiritual master Meher Baba once said that those who live and die unaware of their Real Self, the Indwelling Christ, might as well have been a rock.[316] The 19th-Century American poet Walt Whitman knew all about God in Man:

> Divine am I inside and out, and I make holy whatever I touch or am touch'd from.[317]

WE ARE WHAT JESUS SAID WE ARE

We have now firmly established that, despite all the tortured scripture twisting that John 10:34 has undergone by the unenlightened and ill intentioned, Jesus meant exactly what he said: we are all divine beings, possessing all of the qualities and powers of a supernatural deity. Speaking as the Indwelling One, THE CHRIST, this is precisely what Jesus meant when He said to God (Divine Mind) that "everything I have is yours and everything you have is mine."[318] Or as Paul put it:

> The Spirit itself beareth witness with our spirit, that *we are the children of God*: and if children, then heirs; heirs of God, and joint-heirs with Christ; if so be that we suffer with him, that we may be also *glorified together*.[319]

This is Paul's way of expressing what Jesus so fearlessly proclaimed decades earlier, plainly and simply: "You are all gods"![320]

And here is why this is so. According to our earliest untouched, unedited, intact scriptures (such as The Gospel of Q and The Gospel of Thomas),[321] Jesus was a man[322] who, recognizing that He, like all, possessed the Universal Indwelling Christ,[323] becoming God-realized at the time of his baptism in the Jordan River.[324] Now Christ is God,[325] and God is Universal Love.[326] Therefore, Love is the true King,[327] all of which our Lord confirms for us in *The Aquarian Gospel of Jesus the Christ*:

> . . . all my life was one great drama for the sons of men; a pattern for the sons

of men. I lived to show the possibilities of man. What I have done all men can do, and what I am all men shall be.[328]

Look not upon the flesh; it is not king. *Look to the Christ within who shall be formed in every one of you, as he is formed in me.* When you have purified your hearts by faith, the king will enter in and you will see his face.[329]

"He that hath ears to hear, let him hear."[330] For this is the true "Pearl of Great Price"![331]

Having fully realized THE CHRIST within Himself, our enlightened Lord personified the perfected human being, who came to earth as a shining example of what we were, what we are, and what we might become.

Contrary to popular belief, Jesus did not want attention focused on Himself, the man the New Testament writers not infrequently refer to as the all too mortal "son of Joseph." Thus, to discourage a personality cult in His name, Jesus uttered the now "heterodoxical" words: "*He that believeth on me, believeth not on me, but on him that sent me.*" Rather, our Lord's concentration was, as He says here, always on the Divine Mind (whom He referred to as the "Father," shown on the left), the Holy Spirit (symbolized here in the descending dove), and most especially the human soul, which Jesus called "THE CHRIST" (on the right). According to both the Lord and the Twelve Apostles, all three are one, existing simultaneously in each human being, making us "partakers of the Divine Nature," and "his holiness" as well. And it is for this reason—the reality of our personal Inner Trinity—that Jesus declared to us: "*Ye are gods.*" In the mystical branch of the Church, this is the New Testament's true "Good News," for through our awareness of our divinity, which the ancients knew as God-realization, we grasp that we are immortal, and thus the inheritors of "everlasting life." This is, in turn, connected to the happy Gospel message of Universalism, spelled out in plain language by Saint Luke: "*All flesh* shall see the salvation of God."

3

The Kingdom Within

Part 1

"EVERY MAN IS GOD MADE FLESH"

E HAVE NOW THOROUGHLY DEMONSTRATED that, according to Jesus and numerous ancient Bible authorities, every man is a god and every woman is a goddess, imbued with the same supernatural qualities as God the Father. Shakespeare certainly understood this. Here is how he phrased it in his famous play *Hamlet*:

> What a piece of work is a man, how noble in reason, how infinite in faculties, in form and moving how express and admirable, in action how like an angel, in apprehension *how like a god!*

Yes, you are divine. I am divine. Everyone on earth has a "divine spark" that God instilled in us, linking us one to the other. Known as the Christ Within, or the Indwelling Christ,[332] it is the eternal "high priest"[333] of our personal "church within,"[334] which the Hebraist called the one and only true church, made by the hands of God, not man.[335]

Our unborn, uncreated, immortal, unfathomable, indestructible Inner Christ has existed since the beginning of time,[336] as our Higher Self, the deific human, God in Man,[337] "for every man is God made flesh."[338] This is what Jesus, speaking as the Indwelling Christ, meant when He made the following incredible declaration to his seventy Disciples:

> He that heareth you heareth me; and he that despiseth you despiseth me; and he that despiseth me despiseth him that sent me.[339]

Reread this awe-inspiring passage as many times as you need to until its Truth sinks deep down into your soul!

This is the same Truth that Jesus captured in the following statement: "He that seeth me seeth him that sent me."[340] From a cosmic esoteric perspective, what the Master is saying is this: "When someone looks at you, they are seeing, not you; they are actually seeing God. For the Real You is the Indwelling Christ, and the Indwelling Christ is God."[341] Thus "ye are gods," just as our Lord affirmed.[342]

Yes, it is the Christ Within which makes you divine. Each one of us is a literal individualization of God (Divine Mind), for we have all been created in God's image, perfectly reflecting His glory and power.[343] Thus, the great 13th-Century mystical poet Rumi wrote:

> I looked in temples, churches, and mosques. But I found the divine in my heart.

Paul would have agreed, for according to him, we are each an "anointed" Christ,[344] exact duplicates of the Father.[345] In 1838 Emerson made the following comments in an address before Harvard's Divinity School:

> Jesus Christ belonged to the true race of prophets. He saw with open eye the mystery of the soul. Drawn by its severe harmony, ravished with its beauty, he lived in it, and had his being there. Alone in all history, he estimated the greatness of man. One man was true to what is in you and me. *He saw that God incarnates himself in man*, and evermore goes forth anew to take possession of his world. He said, in this jubilee of sublime emotion, "I am divine. Through me, God acts; through me, speaks. *Would you see God, see me; or, see thee, when thou also thinkest as I now think.*"

MYSTICALLY THE "SECOND COMING" TAKES PLACE WITHIN

Here is the answer to the riddle: Why has no man ever seen God?[346] It is because, as the Apostle John correctly observed, God dwelleth not just outside of us as Invisible Spirit,[347] "God dwelleth *in* us."[348]

Those who come to this realization, of our oneness, our *at-one-ment*, with the "Creator,"[349] have achieved what is often termed "Christ Consciousness," *Kutastha Chaitanya* to Hindus, a psychological state that Paul referred to as "the Mind of Christ."[350] From the mystical Christian point of view, it is through the attainment of Christ Consciousness that we personally experience the Inner Parousia, the spiritual "Second Coming" (of the Christ within).[351] This is why "of that day and that hour knoweth no man, no, not the angels which are in heaven, neither the Son, but the Father."[352]

YOUR DIVINITY MAKES YOU "COMPLETE IN GOD"

Now because the Universal Christ[353] is imbued with "all the fulness of the Godhead bodily,"[354] and because you have the Indwelling Christ,[355] it is clear that you too possess all the powers of the Godhead![356] For we are *"complete in him*, which is the head of all principality and power."[357] Paul, as we saw, had a spectacular way of describing this reality:

> *Let this mind be in you, which was also in Christ Jesus: who, being in the form of God, thought it not robbery to be equal with God.*[358]

How plain the meaning of Paul's statement is: we are supposed to think like Jesus did, namely, that we are "equal with God"! Reread it until you grasp this world-altering message of your divine "completeness" in God.

By following Jesus' teachings, you become a "Son of God," just as He promised,[359] with all of the exalted divine powers that go along with this status, including the ability to find your soulmate, attain happiness, improve your finances, or heal any disease.[360] This is why God said that all things that you decree "shall be established unto thee."[361]

Here is how the Father Himself addressed His earthly devotees on the subject of our divine relationship with Him:

> I will *dwell in them*, and *walk in them*; and I will be their God, and they shall be my people. . . . And [I] will be a Father unto you, and ye shall be my sons and daughters," saith the Lord Almighty.[362]

In The Aquarian Gospel, Jesus elaborates on this topic:

All men are sons of God and if they live a holy life they always are at home with God. They see and understand the works of God, and in his sacred name they can perform these works. . . . The virtues of the heavens are in God's hands, and every loyal son may use these virtues and these powers. Man is the delegate of God to do his will on earth, and man can heal the sick, control the spirits of the air, and raise the dead.

Because I have the power to do these things is nothing strange. All men may gain the power to do these things; but they must conquer all the passions of the lower self; and they can conquer if they will. So *man is God on earth*, and he who honors God must honor man; for *God and man are one, as father and the child are one.* [363]

As Jesus so dramatically proved, the "miracles" He performed, such as spiritual healing, mental telepathy, raising the dead, multiplying physical objects, and bilocation, are possible because we all are "gods on earth"; earthly "Sons" who share a divine connection with the heavenly "Father," the "Unified Field" and "cosmos" of astronomers, which makes up the substance of every particle in the Universe. Indeed, there is only one power, and that power is of God;[364] and there is only one Source, one Energy, one God[365]—and we are all one with it and it is one with all of us.[366] For, as Paul commented, "of him, and through him, and to him, are all things: to whom be glory for ever. Amen [Amon, Amun, Aum, Hum, Om, I AM]."[367]

THE TRUE SELF IS ALL THINGS

Divine Mind's intelligence permeates everything, even what we wrongly call "inanimate" objects. Because of this, every object is sentient on one level or another. In other words, every pebble, every grain of sand, every atom, is alive with the divine intelligence of the One Great Spirit! Truly, as Jesus taught: "God is not the God of the dead, but of the living,"[368] for nothing is truly dead, for nothing can truly "die," including the real you.

Of this inextinguishable infinite substance, the Universal Mind, Emerson once said:

There is one mind common to all individual men. Every man is an inlet to the same and to all of the same. *He that is once admitted to the right of reason is made a freeman of the whole estate.* What Plato has thought, he may think; what a saint has felt, he may feel; what at any time has befallen any man, he can understand. Who hath access to *this universal mind* is a party to all that is or can be done, for *this is the only and sovereign agent*.

In the Upanishads, the Hindus' "Secret Doctrine," we find this delightful scripture:

> And he who beholds *all beings in the Self*, and *the Self in all beings*, he never turns away from it. When to a man who understands, *the Self has become all things*, what sorrow, what trouble can there be to him who once beheld that unity?

Keep in mind the words of Jesus who, speaking as the Indwelling Christ, said: "I am in my Father, and ye in me, and I in you."[369] In plain language the Lord is saying that the Indwelling Christ is in the Divine Mind, the Divine Mind is in the Indwelling Christ, and both are in us!

WE ARE GOD STUFF

Paul asserted in his letter to the Laodiceans that "it is God who worketh *in* you."[370] And it is because of this very fact that we are "partakers of his holiness,"[371] literal "partakers of the divine nature," as Peter put it.[372]

Yes, your Divine Nature makes you a god with divine powers, just as Jesus said![373]

Think of it this way: if God were a vine, we would each be a branch on that vine.[374] If God were a body, we would each be a cell in that body. If God were an ocean, we would each be a drop of water in that ocean. To paraphrase the great astronomer Carl Sagan, we humans are God Stuff.[375] And in fact, God is the Universe, and we are each an atom in that Universe. We are truly all one, spiritually and vibrationally connected by the invisible threads of God Stuff. Of this Doctrine of Oneness, also known as monopsychism, Emerson wrote:

> . . . the universe is represented in every one of its particles. Everything in nature contains all the powers of nature. Everything is made of one hidden stuff. . . . The world globes itself in a drop of dew. The microscope cannot find the animalcule which is less perfect for being little. Eyes, ears, taste, smell, motion, resistance, appetite, and organs of reproduction that take hold on eternity,—all find room to consist in the small creature. . . . The true doctrine of omnipresence is that God appears with all His parts in every moss and cobweb. . . . Thus is the universe alive.[376]

Knowledge of Theosis, the universal Indwelling Christ, long predates Christianity, stretching far back into ancient Pagan Egypt and beyond, as this early illustration of our Lord proves. Though the artist entitled it "Christ Triumphant," it would be more appropriately called "Jesus, God-realized." Like all the savior-sons throughout history, Jesus is shown here emerging from the almond-shaped *Vesica Piscis* ("vessel of the fish"), the universal Pagan female symbol of the Great Virgin Mother-Goddess (Isis, Juno, Hera, Virgo, Mari, etc.). In His left arm He holds the scroll of the true Gospel, which He called "The Gospel of the Kingdom" (and which we know today as The Gospel of Thomas and The Gospel of Q), while in His lap sits the "Holy of Holies," the Sacred Cube, which laid out flat presents a perfect cross, one of the world's great archetypal symbols: its twelve intersecting points and twelve lines signify the twelve Sun-signs of the Zodiac, symbols in turn of the twelve principles or faculties of the human soul (personified as the "Twelve Tribes of Israel" in the Old Testament and the "Twelve Apostles" in the New Testament). The four arms of the cross stand for the sacred number four, symbol of the material plane. The cube's three visible sides signify the sacred number three, symbol of the spiritual plane. When four and three are added, they equal the most holy of all numbers, seven, the number-symbol of Theosis: *Spirit implanted in Material*, that is, God in Man, or what we know as THE CHRIST. Jesus here is surrounded by the Christian Tetramorph, the Four Gospelers, who began life in ancient Egypt as "The Fathers": the four fixed signs of the Zodiac, emblems in turn of the Four Elements, which, written in Hebrew, are: *Iammin* ("water"), *Nour* ("fire"), *Rouach* ("air"), and *Iebeschah* ("earth"). The first letter of each word gives us the esoteric acronym INRI, which in mystical Latin stands for *In Nobis Regnat Iesus* ("Within Us Reigns Jesus"). The four astrological Pagan "Fathers" of the Tetramorph were selected by the Church Father Irenaeus (a proponent of Theosis) to symbolize the Evangelists of the four Gospels which he chose for inclusion in the New Testament: in the upper left corner we have *Matthew* as Aquarius the Water Bearer; in the upper right we have *John* as Aquila the Eagle (later known as Scorpio); in the lower left corner there is *Mark* as Leo the Lion; and in the lower right *Luke* as Taurus the Bull—all, like Jesus, holding the Sacred Cube. (The Pagan Tetramorph also appears in Jewish mythology in the book of Ezekiel as the Cherubim, or "four living creatures.") For those who require further proof of Christianity's adoption of the doctrine of Theosis from earlier Pagan religions, take a tour of the ancient cathedrals of Europe. Here, in such magnificent places as France's Chartres Cathedral, one can still see countless stained glass and carved stone images of the Christian Tetramorph, the theosistic cruciform symbol of God in Man: THE CHRIST.

THE KINGDOM OF GOD EXISTS HERE & NOW

Because we are earthly deities, co-heirs[377] of the Father's divine inheritance,[378] we have been given one of the greatest gifts imaginable: the ability to do what Jesus called "enter into the Kingdom of God."[379]

What exactly is the Kingdom of God, the Kingdom of Heaven, or the "portable paradise,"[380] as it is also known?

Mainstream Christianity teaches that it is a place in Heaven where good Christians go *after* they die. However, this is not what Jesus taught. According to His own words, the Kingdom of God exists *right now here on earth*; not as a physical abode, but as a psychological one. Here is how he phrased it:

> My kingdom is not of this world.[381] [Thus,] neither shall they say, "Lo here!" or, "lo there!" for, behold, *the kingdom of God is within you*.[382]

Speaking as the Indwelling Christ, here is the inner meaning of these scriptures:

> The Kingdom of God is not a material place. It is a spiritual, that is, a psychological one. So if someone tries to tell you that the Kingdom is a specific physical site located somewhere on earth or that it can only be entered in the Afterlife, do not believe them. For it is located inside of you right now, deep within that aspect of you that is connected to the Father, or Divine Mind: your Higher Self, which is known as THE CHRIST.[383]

One of our Savior's favorite expressions was "the kingdom of heaven is at hand."[384] The dictionary states that at hand means "something that is occurring right now," something that is "within easy reach." This is why Jesus always referred to the Kingdom of Heaven in the *present tense*, asserting that it is "at hand,"[385] and this is why we find this dialogue in The Gospel of Thomas:

> Jesus' Disciples asked him: "When are the dead going to finally rest, and precisely when is the New World going to arrive?" He replied: "What you are seeking has already come, but you do not know it."[386]

In other words, the Kingdom of God is not in the past or in the future, but rather it is happening at this very moment.[387] And there is only one way that this could be possible: it exists *within you* as a psychological state of mind.[388] This is why "every man presseth into it" (that is, the wise seek the kingdom with great enthusiasm)—just as Jesus said![389]

OUR AT-ONE-MENT WITH THE FATHER

Achieving this state of mind, or what Jesus esoterically called "entering the Kingdom of God,"[390] has been given many names, including: enlightenment, salvation, gnosis, nirvana, satori, epiphany, bodhi, theophany, theaphany, mar'eh, hierophany, tapas, kensho, Abraham Consciousness, Moses Consciousness, Chrishna Consciousness, Chrishnahood, Buddha Consciousness, Buddhahood, Christhood, Cosmic Consciousness, self-realization, ananda, sat-chit-ananda, moksa, hazon, kaivalya, christophany, mukti, yogasema, apavarga, darshan, sukha, fana, illumination, turiya, samadhi, and the Perfect.[391]

What do such arcane words and phrases mean to you and me on a personal level? Generally speaking, all indicate the same thing: the realization that our Higher Self, the omnipresent indestructible Indwelling Christ, is one with God, for Jesus said not only are we one with God,[392] we literally are gods.[393]

Understanding our oneness, that is, our *at-one-ment*, with the "Creator,"[394] and knowing this with full undeviating faith, is enlightenment, true salvation! As the ancient Christians said, "if the soul were not essentially Godlike, it could never know God."[395] Jesus possessed this knowledge, this high, pure, spiritual state of consciousness, and we are to seek it and possess it as well. Thus the Thirteenth Apostle commanded us to "arm yourselves with the same mind" as the Lord.[396]

ALL ARE INVITED INTO THE KINGDOM

Indeed, Jesus asserted that all men and women are invited into the Kingdom Within. Thus, He compared the Kingdom of God (in Greek, *Basileia tou Theou*) to a wedding feast in which the king tells his servants:

> Go ye therefore into the highways, and as many as ye shall find, bid to the marriage.[397]

In another passage Jesus says:

And I say unto you, that many shall come from the east and west, and shall sit down with Abraham, and Isaac, and Jacob, in the kingdom of heaven.[398]

Paul too reminded us that the Father has openly called all of His children to share in His Kingdom and in His "glory" (divine powers):

As ye know how we exhorted and comforted and charged every one of you, as a father doth his children, that ye would walk worthy of God, who hath called you unto his kingdom and glory.[399]

SEEK THE KINGDOM & THE ABUNDANT LIFE WILL BE YOURS
What is so important about "entering the Kingdom of God"? Why should it matter to us?

The answer is that it is part of God's great plan for us here on earth, for Jesus promised that those who are able to enter the Kingdom of God will be able to live carefree lives filled with abundance, health, and happiness; lives without worry, fear, hunger, or poverty. Peter put it this way: "Cast all your cares upon God, for he careth for you."[400]

In The Gospel of Judas, Jesus calls this high level of consciousness—which we know as the Kingdom of God or Heaven—a "great and boundless realm." And it truly is! It is the "secret place of the most High" mentioned in the Old Testament, and those who "dwell" here "shall abide under the shadow of the Almighty," where "no evil shall befall them."[401] Here is how the Psalmist phrased it:

The Lord [God the Father, Divine Mind] is my shepherd; *I shall not want*. He maketh me to lie down in green pastures: he leadeth me beside the still waters. He restoreth my soul: he leadeth me in the paths of righteousness for his name's sake. Yea, though I walk through the valley of the shadow of death, *I will fear no evil*: for thou art with me; thy rod and thy staff they comfort me. Thou preparest a table before me in the presence of mine enemies: thou anointest my head with oil; *my cup runneth over*. *Surely goodness and mercy shall follow me all the days of my life*: and I will dwell in the house of the Lord for ever.[402]

Yes, if you "dwell in the house of the Lord" (the Kingdom of Heaven) you shall "not want," you shall "fear no evil," your "cup will runneth over," all of your desires will manifest, and you will want for nothing. As Paul said:

God hath not given us the spirit of fear; but of power, and of love, and of a sound mind.[403]

This "sound mind" is the Divine Mind, which Jesus called the "Father," and which—due to the Law of Attraction—is always outwardly expressing our most dominant inner thoughts on the material plane. Consider the words of the Savior:

> Therefore I say unto you, take no thought for your life, what ye shall eat, or what ye shall drink; nor yet for your body, what ye shall put on. Is not the life more than meat, and the body than raiment? Behold the fowls of the air: for they sow not, neither do they reap, nor gather into barns; yet your heavenly Father feedeth them. Are ye not much better than they? Which of you by taking thought can add one cubit unto his stature?
>
> And why take ye thought for raiment? Consider the lilies of the field, how they grow; they toil not, neither do they spin: and yet I say unto you, that even Solomon in all his glory was not arrayed like one of these. Wherefore, if God so clothe the grass of the field, which to day is, and to morrow is cast into the oven, shall he not much more clothe you, O ye of little faith?
>
> Therefore take no thought, saying, "what shall we eat?" or, "what shall we drink?" or, "wherewithal shall we be clothed?" (For after all these things do the Gentiles [nonbelievers] seek:) for your heavenly Father knoweth that ye have need of all these things. But *seek ye first the kingdom of God, and his righteousness; and all these things shall be added unto you.*[404]

ENTERING THE KINGDOM GIVES US UNLIMITED POWER

What a pledge Jesus has made to us. When we "enter" the Kingdom of God, the realm of Divine Mind, we realize not only our personal divinity and oneness with God, but our amazing divine powers as well; powers that enable us to create any kind of life we want for ourselves and for our loved ones through our faith and thoughts!

We discover, in fact, that our Higher Self, our Divine Self, the Indwelling Christ,[405] makes us the king[406] of our own personal kingdom within![407] This is why the Master gave us this glorious formula:

> What things soever ye desire, when ye pray, believe that ye receive them, and ye shall have them.[408]

How is it possible that we possess such power, the Godlike power to "receive what things soever we desire"?

It is due to the fact that when we are operating out of the inner realm of THE CHRIST, the Kingdom of God, our divine powers are fully activated. Thus, it is at this time that not only do we have maximum spiritual control over our physical lives (health, wealth, happiness, etc.), but the physical plane has the least effect upon us in return. Combined with positive thoughts and pure unqualified faith, our prayer-desires contain the limitless ability to create the life of our choosing![409]

RIGHT-LIVING IS YOUR TICKET INTO THE KINGDOM

Think about all of this for a moment. Now you understand why Jesus preached what He called "the Gospel of the Kingdom"[410] instead of "the Gospel of Jesus Christ" (which was preached only by those who came after Him);[411] now you know why His focus was always on the "Father" (Divine Mind)[412] and the "Son" (the Indwelling Christ),[413] rather than on Himself as the human Jesus.[414]

Now you see why He asked us to "obey" His commandments.[415] Not to please the capricious, overly critical, Paganesque, and often sadistic and violent God of the Old Testament[416]—which He overturned and replaced with a God of love.[417] But because "as a man thinketh in his heart, so is he," as the Proverbist affirmed.[418] In other words, *living right, thinking right, speaking right, and acting right is what grants us entrance into the here-and-now Kingdom of Heaven,*[419] where anything and everything is possible through the mind alone![420] "If ye do these things," as Peter said,

> ye shall never fall: for so an entrance shall be ministered unto you abundantly into the everlasting kingdom of our Lord and Saviour Jesus Christ.[421]

This is why Paul says that due to our union with the Indwelling Christ, we are "enriched" in all things.[422]

In The Aquarian Gospel the Lord further elucidates upon this topic:

> The news spread through the city and along the shore that Judah's king had come, and multitudes drew near to press his hand. And Jesus said, "I cannot show the king, unless you see with eyes of soul, because *the kingdom of the king is in the soul. And every soul a kingdom is.* There is a king for every man. *This king is love, and when this love becomes the greatest power in life, it is the Christ; so Christ is king. And every one may have this Christ dwell in his soul, as Christ dwells*

in my soul."[423]

A RADICAL PERSONAL INNER JOURNEY

Although everyone is invited to the "feast" of the Kingdom of God, only a handful will actually attend, for "many are called, but few are chosen."[424] The truth is, as Jesus stated, that not even being a Christian will necessarily grant one entrance into the Kingdom:

> Not every one that saith unto me, "Lord, Lord," shall enter into the kingdom of heaven; but he that doeth the will of my Father which is in heaven. Many will say to me in that day, "Lord, Lord, have we not prophesied in thy name? and in thy name have cast out devils? and in thy name done many wonderful works?" And then will I profess unto them, "I never knew you: depart from me, ye that work iniquity."[425]

Indeed, not only did the Master say that individuals from both the East (that is, Pagans) and the West (Christians) would one day sit down together in the Kingdom of Heaven,[426] but the lowest outcasts of society would enter it before the literal minded, overly strict, intolerant, prejudiced, judgmental, formalistic "Pharisees" of Christianity.[427]

The reason for this is that entering the Kingdom of God (realizing our at-one-ment with God—which Origen referred to as "spiritual Christianity" as opposed to what I call "religious Christianity")—is an intensely personal journey that requires one to undergo a radical transformation of personality, one that awakens the spiritual conscious from its unconscious slumber.

To put it another way, it is a highly private, individualistic endeavor, requiring diligence, sacrifice, and dedication to a new way of thinking, a new way of acting, a new way of speaking; in truth, an entirely new way of life. This is what Paul meant when he said that "*we must through much tribulation enter into the kingdom of God.*"[428]

This sometimes difficult refining process is what separates the wheat (the dedicated) from the chaff (the insincere), proving ourselves worthy of entrance into this most sacred realm[429]—one that was so important to Jesus that He dedicated the majority of His later life and teachings to it.[430]

Indeed, totally giving up one's old life to the Great I AM Presence Within[431] is the only way to attain the Kingdom and realize our divinity.

It is the equivalent of an inner revolution of body, mind, and spirit, in which our former unspiritual life (which was led by the Ego or "Satan") is "killed" off, replaced by a brand new life in Christ (led by the Divine Mind or "God"). Thus Paul said:

> I am crucified with Christ: nevertheless I live; yet not I, but *Christ liveth in me*: and the life which I now live in the flesh I live by the faith of the Son of God, who loved me, and gave himself for me.[432]

"TAKING UP YOUR CROSS"
In mystical Christianity this transition to allowing "Christ to live in you" is symbolized in the image of the crucifixion of the selfish atheistic "I," the Ego, on the cross: we figuratively "kill off" our old egocentric life and its leader the Human Mind, and substitute it with a spiritcentric life headed by the Divine Mind, which Jesus called the "Father."[433] Psychologically, this is what our Lord meant by the following:

> Whosoever will come after me, let him deny himself, and take up his cross, and follow me. For whosoever will save his [ego-centered] life shall lose it; but whosoever shall lose his [ego-centered] life for my sake and the gospel's [of the Kingdom of God], the same shall save it. For what shall it profit a man, if he shall gain the whole world [materially], and lose his own soul [that is, lose touch with his own Indwelling Christ]?[434]

If you are serious about entering the Kingdom of God, the Realm of Divine Mind, you must follow the Indwelling Christ.[435] This means forfeiting your former ego-guided life for a new Spirit-led life; for the vain, shallow, dualistic Ego (which sees itself as being separate from God) is little more than conceit and narcissism, the opposite of the all-giving Father. "Vanity of vanities, saith the preacher; all is vanity."[436]

REQUIREMENTS FOR GAINING ACCESS TO THE KINGDOM
In his second letter the Apostle Peter clearly lays out the requisites for entrance into the "everlasting" Inner Kingdom:

> . . . giving all diligence, add to your faith virtue; and to virtue knowledge; and to knowledge temperance; and to temperance patience; and to patience godliness; and to godliness brotherly kindness; and to brotherly kindness charity. For if these things be in you, and abound, they make you that ye shall

neither be barren nor unfruitful in the knowledge [Gnosis] of our Lord Jesus Christ. But he that lacketh these things is [spiritually] blind, and cannot see afar off [the Truth], and hath forgotten that *he was purged from his old sins.* Wherefore . . . rather, brethren, give diligence to make your calling and election sure: for if ye do these things, ye shall never fall: for so *an entrance shall be ministered unto you abundantly into the everlasting kingdom of our Lord and Saviour Jesus Christ.*[437]

Peter tells us that to gain entrance we must strive for the pristine state of consciousness possessed by Jesus Himself. Call it what you will: Abraham Consciousness, Moses Consciousness, Cosmic Consciousness, Chrishna Consciousness, or Christ Consciousness,[438] it is a state that *anyone* can attain—if he or she is willing to work at it—due to the Universal Christ Within.[439]

LIVING & DYING IN CHRIST

Listen closely. This is the key to your light (enlightenment) and your salvation (well-being).[440] We must give ourselves over entirely to the Indwelling Christ, our Divine Author and Perfecter,[441] and we begin this process by "crucifying" (dissolving) the Ego (which Paul called "the flesh"),[442] a spiritual act that Zen Buddhists refer to as the "Great Death."

As Paul did, we must nail our "I" to the cross[443] before we can recognize the "Christ who liveth in us."[444] This is what the Thirteenth Apostle meant when he made the following mystical statement: "For to me to live is Christ, and to die is gain."[445] The inner meaning:

> To me life is the Indwelling Christ, my Higher Self; thus the death of its opposite, my Lower Self, my Ego, is a victory.[446]

To "live and die in Christ" requires a complete renewal of the mind, or what Jesus referred to as being spiritually "born again": the "death" of our old consciousness—called the "old man" by Paul[447]—and the "birth" of a new consciousness—called the "new man" by Paul.[448] Why is this necessary?

God does not change Himself to suit us. We must change ourselves to suit God, the Father, Divine Mind! The Medieval mystics taught that "love changes the lover into the beloved." How true. In his letter to the Romans, here is how Paul explained it:

And *be not conformed to this world* [mass mind, i.e., society]: but *be ye transformed by the renewing of your mind*, that ye may prove what is that good, and acceptable, and perfect, will of God.[449]

Once we have "renewed our mind" by the "crucifixion" of our Lower Self on the spiritual cross, that part of us "dies." We have truly "overcome the Wicked One," as John put it.[450] Our Higher Self is then "risen" and brought under the protection of the Divine Mind.

Here is how Paul phrased this concept in the flowery language of my cousin, the Medieval King James:

If *ye then be risen with Christ*, seek those things which are above, where Christ sitteth on the right hand of God. Set your affection on things above [on the Higher Self], not on things on the earth [on the Lower Self]. For ye [your Egos] are dead, and your life is hid with [the Indwelling] Christ in God [Divine Mind].[451]

Isaiah gave us this message about mental renewal, also contrasting the Lower Self with the Higher Self:

Seek ye the Lord [Divine Mind] while he may be found, call ye upon him while he is near: let the wicked forsake his way, and the unrighteous man his thoughts: and let him return unto the Lord, and he will have mercy upon him; and to our God, for he will abundantly pardon. "For my [the Higher Self's] thoughts are not your [the Lower Self's] thoughts, neither are your ways my ways," saith the Lord. "For as the heavens are higher than the earth, so are my ways higher than your ways, and my thoughts than your thoughts."[452]

The artist titled this illustration, "Jesus healing the blind." But according to Jesus Himself, he did not heal anyone. In nearly every case, after the cure was effected, the Lord told his patient: "Be happy, *your* faith has made you whole." Thus the Master said that due to our Divine Nature, "*he that believeth on me, the works that I do shall he do also; and greater works than these shall he do.*" In other words, the Indwelling Christ provides us with the power to heal any disease by altering biology and compacting time. Do you doubt or do you believe? Jesus said: "Fear not: believe only"!

4

The Kingdom Within

Part 2

THE MYSTICAL SIGNIFICANCE OF THE HOLY CROSS

T SHOULD BE CLEAR BY now why the Lord gave us the following commandment. Read it not with your tuitive (logical) mind, but with your Inner Eye, your spiritual eye, which Hindus call the "Third Eye" and which Jesus called "the light of the body."[453] I am speaking of your intuition:

> If any man will come after me, let him deny himself, and take up his cross daily, and follow me. [454]

Now read this esoteric statement by Barnabas: "Blessed are they who put their trust in the cross."[455]

Why are these statements so important? What is it about the cross that is so vital to our spiritual growth as Christians? The orthodox branch of the Church has its literal answer to these questions, and with this well-known mainstream dogma we have no quarrel.

However, the mystical branch of the Church has its own answer, albeit one that must be interpreted by each individual as their personal level of spiritual consciousness allows. And here we will reveal one of the greatest occult secrets of all time.

The cross is not a Christian symbol specifically, of course. It was not even adopted by the Church until the 7th Century, and it did not become authorized for official use until the 9th Century.[456] In fact, the cross is not only a universal emblem, it is the most universal of all symbols,[457] one found as far back as 35,000 years ago in the cave art of Cro-Magnon man. And it has been used in the religions and myths of every people, society, and civilization ever since, from the pre-Christian Hindus, Egyptians, Greeks, and Scandinavians, to the pre-Christian Chinese, Celts, Romans, and Native-Americans[458]—most traditionally as a symbol of the World-Axis or Tree of Life.[459]

Not surprisingly, during the time of Jesus the cross was a common symbol among both Pagans and Jews, the latter who enigmatically symbolized it in the obscure design known as the "Holy of Holies."[460] What is the true nature of this, the cryptic *Sanctum Sanctorum*?

It is a six-sided cube (in ancient times often idealized as a perfectly square temple),[461] which, when cut open and laid flat, presents a crucifix with *four arms* (symbols of the four fixed signs of the Zodiac, the four elements, the four directions, the four seasons, the four ages of the world, the four suits in a card deck, the four parts of Jesus' garments divided by the Roman soldiers, the four living creatures of Ezekiel, the four horns, angels, and beasts of Revelation, the four corners of the earth, the four Gospels, etc.) and *twelve lines* and *twelve intersecting points* (symbols of the twelve star-signs, the twelve months of the year, the twelve hours each of daylight and nighttime, the twelve years of Jesus' childhood, the Twelve Tribes of Israel, the Twelve Patriarchs, the twelve gates, foundations, angels, fruits, and pearls of Revelation, the Twelve Apostles, etc.).

WHY THE ANCIENTS CALLED THE HUMAN EGO "SATAN"

As mentioned, the reader must interpret these arcane facts as he or she will. What is most important, however, is this: until we have achieved total Christ Consciousness, we must renew our mind on a daily basis. Why? In great part, this is due to our old negative programming, harmful ideas instilled in our minds over many years by the mass mind (the aggregate of society's most common everyday concepts, thoughts, fears, misconceptions, and ideas). These destructive beliefs, stored in our Subconscious, have become so deeply embedded that only by repeated effort (right-thinking, right-speaking, and right action)[462] can we eliminate them.[463]

But there is another reason we need to refresh our minds everyday as well: the persistent and stubborn nature of the Ego. Our Ego cannot imagine earthly life without itself, for being "Satanic" it is self-centered, self-assertive, self-absorbed, and self-interested, and being dualistic it perceives itself as an independent god in its own right—completely separate from God the Father.

Being innately irresponsible, our Ego cannot tolerate the idea that, as divine beings whose thoughts are creating our daily lives moment by moment, we are responsible for everything that happens to us.[464] Seeing itself as pitiable, isolated, downtrodden, sad, and contemptible, it feels unworthy of all the good things in life, such as perfect health, wealth, and happiness. Perceiving itself as inadequate, guilt-ridden, insecure, and pessimistic, it fabricates feelings of low self-esteem in order to confirm its own poor self image.

Knowing that it is mortal and that it will pass into nothingness when our God-Self sheds our physical body,[465] our Ego fears death above all. Finally, and most damaging to us, there is the Ego's belief that being tiny, weak, powerless, and insignificant, it must utterly reject Jesus' teaching that we are gods, with access to all of the same powers as the Father.[466]

So our Ego-Self, our human spirit, fights our God-Self, the Holy Spirit, at every turn, constantly struggling to combat Divine principles, Divine teachings, Divine Truth, putting as much distance between itself and the Almighty as possible. This is the true meaning of Paul's often misunderstood statement:

> For the wages of sin is death, but the gift of God is eternal life through Jesus Christ our Lord.[467]

The inner meaning:

> The "payment" we receive for wrong thought, wrong speech, and wrong action—that is, living from out of the Lower Self or Ego—is separation from the Divine Mind. But those who live from out of the Indwelling Christ—that is, the Higher Self—are rewarded with permanent oneness with the Divine Mind, where anything and everything is possible.[468]

It is little wonder that the ancients referred to the powerful and voracious human Ego esoterically as the "Devil," "Satan," "Lucifer," and the "Adversary." It represents the "bad guy" in the archetypal battle between good and evil, light and darkness, that is at the heart of so many books, films, plays, TV shows, poems, operas, computer games, and songs.

THE INWARD MAN VS. THE OUTWARD MAN

Paul often spoke of this eternal conflict between the Ego/Lower Self, or what he called the "outward man," and THE CHRIST/Higher Self, or what he termed the "inward man":[469]

> For I know that in me (that is, in my flesh [Lower Self],) dwelleth no good thing: for to will is present with me; but how to perform that which is good I find not. For the good that I would I do not: but the evil which I would not, that I do. Now if I do that I would not, it is no more I that do it, but sin that dwelleth in me. I find then a law, that, when I would do good, evil is present with me.
>
> For I delight in the law of God after the *inward man* [Higher Self]: but I see another law in my members [body], warring against the law of my mind [Conscious Mind], and bringing me into captivity to the law of sin which is in my members. O wretched man that I am! who shall deliver me from the body of this death [that is, spiritual separation from Divine Mind]? I thank God through Jesus Christ our Lord [that is, for the Indwelling Christ or Higher Self]. So then with the mind [Conscious Mind] I myself serve the law of God [Divine Mind]; but with the flesh [Ego/Lower Self] the law of sin [wrong-thinking].[470]

With your new understanding of the human Ego, read the following statement by Peter:

> Be sober, be vigilant; because your adversary the devil, as a roaring lion, walketh about, seeking whom he may devour.[471]

Acclaimed motivational author and speaker Dr. Wayne Dyer teaches that Ego is an acronym for "Edging God out," and he is correct. And it is for this reason that we must hang it on the cross and "crucify" it everyday, pushing back the human (the "outward man") to make way for the divine ("inward man").

DYING DAILY IN THE LORD

Now you know what Paul meant when he said "in Jesus Christ our Lord, I die daily,"[472] and "for thy sake we are killed all the day long."[473] He is not talking about physical death, but rather the psychological end of our former ways of thinking, which he personified as the crucified "old man" or "outward man" (Lower Self), and its replacement of a new risen spirit, the "new man" or "inward man" (Higher Self).

Thus, as the Lower Self (connected with our physical body) decreases in power, the Higher Self (connected with our spiritual body) increases in power, just as the saint tells us in his second letter to the Jesus community at Corinth:

> For which cause we faint not; but though our *outward man* perish, yet the *inward man* is renewed day by day.[474]

And in his letter to his followers at Ephesus, Paul says:

> That ye put off concerning the former conversation the *old man* [the old consciousness of your Lower Self], which is corrupt according to the deceitful lusts; and be renewed in the spirit of your mind ["the Mind of Christ"]; and that ye put on the *new man* [the new consciousness of your Higher Self], which after God [Divine Mind] is created in righteousness and true holiness.[475]

ACKNOWLEDGING THE INDWELLING CHRIST

In order to gain membership into the Kingdom, you must not only "renew your mind" and "put on the new man" that is created in God's image,[476] you must also be willing to leave behind everyone who is not ready to embark on their own inner journey. But whoever accepts you also accepts the Holy Christ Within, and whoever accepts the Holy Christ Within accepts the Father, Divine Mind, as well. So saith our Lord Jesus, who, as He so often did, speaks here as the Indwelling Christ:

> Whosoever therefore shall confess [that is, acknowledge] me [the Indwelling Christ] before men, him will I confess also before my Father which is in heaven [Divine Mind]. But whosoever shall deny me before men, him will I also deny before my Father which is in heaven. Think not that I am come to send peace on earth: I came not to send peace, but a sword. For I am come to set a man at variance against his father, and the daughter against her

mother, and the daughter in law against her mother in law. And a man's foes shall be they of his own household.

He that loveth father or mother more than me is not worthy of me [the Indwelling Christ]: and he that loveth son or daughter more than me is not worthy of me. And he that taketh not his cross [does not crucify his Ego], and followeth after me, is not worthy of me [will never achieve oneness with the Christ Within].

He that findeth his life shall lose it [he who tries to preserve his Ego will be miserable]: and he that loseth his life for my sake shall find it [he who "kills" his Ego for the purpose of attaining "the Mind of Christ" will be happy]. He that receiveth [accepts] you receiveth me, and he that receiveth me receiveth him that sent me [God, Divine Mind].[477]

As Jesus notes, this psychological process of violently overthrowing the Ego, the "old man," the old ways of thinking, in order to enter the Kingdom was actually well-known at one time, particularly during the 1st Century, the period in which He lived on earth:

And from the days of John the Baptist until now the kingdom of heaven suffereth violence, and the violent take it by force.[478]

PUTTING NEW WINE INTO NEW BOTTLES

Still, this type of complete crisis of consciousness, that is, "putting on the new man," is necessary for entrance into the Kingdom, as Jesus states:

No man putteth a piece of new cloth unto an old garment, for that which is put in to fill it up taketh from the garment, and the rent is made worse. Neither do men put new wine into old bottles: else the bottles break, and the wine runneth out, and the bottles perish: but they put new wine into new bottles, and both are preserved.[479]

The inner meaning:

No sane person tries to fit a new concept into an outdated belief system, for it will only weaken the belief system further. Or put another way, a low consciousness thought cannot be contained in a high consciousness mind, and a high consciousness thought cannot be contained in a low consciousness mind. In other words, in order to enter the Kingdom of Divine Mind, one must become spiritually enlightened, which requires discarding the old unspiritual ways of thinking.[480]

In The Aquarian Gospel, Jesus puts it this way:

> Old wine may be preserved in ancient skins; but new wine calls for bottles new. This spirit-truth I bring is to this generation new, and if we put it in the ancient skins of [fundamentalist, orthodox] Jewish forms, lo, it will all be lost. It must expand; the ancient bottles cannot yield and they would burst. Behold the kingdom of the Christ! it is as old as God himself, and yet it is as new as morning sun; it only can contain the truth of God.[481]

NONCONFORMITY & THE KINGDOM OF HEAVEN

Of course, not everyone is interested in putting "new wine into new bottles," of forcefully overturning their Ego, their old patterns of thinking, their entire worldview. When one embarks on the road less traveled, the individual path to Godhood, it takes a fearless and totally committed nonconformist, one who understands that this lonely and sometimes perilous inner journey leads to a paradise of splendor and unfathomable rewards. For:

> Eye hath not seen, nor ear heard, neither have entered into the heart of man, the things which God hath prepared for them that love him.[482]

Who then would not look forward to drinking the "new wine" with Jesus in the Father's Kingdom?[483]

Sadly, as is the case today, in Jesus' time many Christians were conformists who much preferred being part of a collective group, one in which they could remain spiritually unconscious, while their pastor interpreted scripture for them and told them what to think, what to say, and what to do.

Hence, though Jesus invited everyone to enter the Kingdom of God and discover their astonishing self-creative powers for themselves, very few take Him up on the offer. Fear, apathy, the mass mind, and the herd mentality make it much easier for the average Christian to remain part of his church group instead of striking out on his own—which is what Jesus and the Kingdom require. "Be not conformed to this world," said Paul.[484] For when it comes to living in the Spirit, conformity is death, individualism is life! One of our most enlightened Christian brothers, Emerson, once wrote: "Do not go where the path may lead, go instead where there is no path and leave a trail."

The Cross means one thing to the institutionalized Church, and quite another to the mystical branch of Christianity. Ancient Christian mystic Paul viewed each story, event, figure, and object in the Bible as an "allegory," and so does the modern Christian mystic. The Thirteenth Apostle said, "in Christ I die daily" and "for thy sake we are killed all the day long." He cannot be talking about actual physical death on a real crucifix. He is referring to a mystical one, that is, a psychological one; and so it is, for psychology means "the science of the Soul," and the Soul is just another word for THE CHRIST. To "enter the Kingdom of God" one's Ego must be crucified on the Cross of Love, releasing The Christ-Soul so that it may pass through the Straight Gate at the entrance. This requires one to be "born again" (overthrow one's former ways of thinking) and achieve the *Hieros Gamos* ("Sacred Union"): a perfect balance between the Male Principle (the conscious mind) and the Female Principle (the subconscious mind). There are symbolized in the Sun and Moon images at the top of the cross above—which Jesus called "serpents" and "doves" respectively. It is our Divine Nature that gives us the ability to recognize the Kingdom Within, and it is the Christlike life that grants us entrance.

GOD LOVES INDIVIDUALS NOT RELIGION!

If you want to please God, "render unto Caesar the things which be Caesar's" (that is, always follow the legal and accepted standards and laws of your country),[485] but *care not what others think*. Do not imitate anyone, ignore societal trends. Instead, strike out on your own, think for yourself, develop your own style, your own philosophies, your own views. You are here to discover yourself, your divinity, and to forge your own road toward oneness with God, whatever you image Him/Her/It to be. New Thought leader Prentice Mulford once said:

> In the spiritual life every person is his or her own discoverer, and you need not grieve if your discoveries are not believed by others.

Jesus was the world's ultimate independent thinker and nonconformist, one who not only refused to be squeezed into the rigid mold of either traditional religion or society, but who taught that each person is a completely unique god or goddess,[486] imbued with their own divine powers.[487] No wonder both His conformist critics and even His close friends thought He was a madman, possessed by the Devil![488]

WHAT IT MEANS TO "ENTER AT THE STRAIT GATE"

Jesus dealt with the social consequences of His nonconformity by spending as much time in solitude as He could, away from the bustling towns, far from the madding crowds and the needy crush of His many followers.[489] Here is how the Master answered the question: should we conform to religion and society or not?

> Enter ye in at the strait gate: for wide is the gate, and broad is the way, that leadeth to destruction, and many there be which go in thereat: Because strait is the gate, and narrow is the way, which leadeth unto life, and few there be that find it.[490]

Here is the modern inner interpretation:

> There are two gates before you: one leading to the Kingdom of Heaven, the other to the Kingdom of Hell. Which one will you choose? I am asking you to choose the gate to the Kingdom of Heaven. But few of you will do so, for the entranceway to the Kingdom of Heaven is narrow and uncomfortable, and its pathway is cluttered with obstacles; meaning that in order to get in, you

will have to undergo an inner and sometimes painful personal trial that completely changes your consciousness. Thus, most of you will choose the gate to the Kingdom of Hell, because its entranceway is wide and its pathway is open and clear; meaning that, because there is no change of consciousness required, it is much easier to get in. But be forewarned: the comfortable path to the Kingdom of Hell leads to personal misery![491]

The gate of the Kingdom of Heaven is so narrow that we must go through single file, one person at a time. Yet the gate of the Kingdom of Hell is so wide that an entire group of people can go through at once. The former gate is for individualists and nonconformists, the latter gate is for groups and conformists!

WHO IS MOST LIKELY TO ENTER THE KINGDOM OF GOD?

It is precisely because of the difficulty of entering the Kingdom of Heaven that the poor, the downtrodden, the sick, the humble, the simple, the modest, the uneducated, the traumatized, the undesirable, the inferior, the injured, the unrighteous, the unpopular, the lonely, and the pariahs of society are most likely to seek entrance. They have much less to lose and much more to gain than the rich, the powerful, the healthy, the self-sufficient, the righteous, the educated, and the popular members of society. This is why Jesus said:

> Blessed are the poor in spirit: for theirs is the kingdom of heaven. . . . Blessed are they which are persecuted for righteousness' sake: for theirs is the kingdom of heaven.[492]

The Lord was very well aware that the lowliest would usually enter the Kingdom of God before the most honored of society (in His day, the fundamentalist Pharisees):

> Jesus saith unto them, "Verily I say unto you, that the publicans [tax collectors] and the harlots [prostitutes] go into the kingdom of God before you."[493]

Indeed, God's radical Kingdom turns the normal world upside down:

> But many that are first shall be last; and the last shall be first.[494]

From such statements it is clear that the Father, Divine Mind, did not create His kingdom, the Kingdom of God, for groups, churches, or religions. And it is for this very fact that you will never hear this truth being advocated from the pulpit at Sunday School!

Yet, Paul understood this truth, which is why he preached against the formation of "strife [partisanship], seditions [divisions], and heresies [following the beliefs of the Ego/Satan]," assuring us that "they which do such things shall not inherit the kingdom of God."[495]

WHY JESUS COMPARED THE KINGDOM TO A MUSTARD SEED

Just as importantly, the Kingdom is not understandable through the intellect,[496] it is not set in the future, and it is not located anywhere on the physical plane, as we have been wrongly taught. The Kingdom of God was designed strictly for the individual, it exists in the here and now, and it must be discovered through *one-on-one experience* of the Divine; personal self-reflection that results in *direct knowledge* (Gnosis) of the Supreme Being. Why?

Because, as Jesus said: "The Kingdom of God is *within you*,"[497] not within a group, an organization, or a religion. Just you.

Thus in our busy world today the Kingdom goes completely unnoticed by most people: like God Himself, it is immanent and invisible,[498] and yet it is so fragile that only through a perfect balance between mind, body, and spirit can we access it.[499] It is so seemingly inconsequential, even to many Christian authorities, that Jesus compared it to two of the world's smallest and most humble objects: a mustard seed and a grain of bread yeast.[500]

Though, because it is not perceptible to human eyes the Kingdom seems insignificant to many, Jesus teaches us that it is so important that we are to try and obtain it before and above all other things: "Seek ye first the kingdom of God."[501] And here, according to the Master, is why:

> Verily I say unto you, there is no man that hath left house, or parents, or brethren, or wife, or children, for the kingdom of God's sake, who shall not receive manifold more *in this present time*, and in the world to come life everlasting.[502]

SPIRITUAL REBIRTH & CONVERSION

Merely following Jesus' teachings *intellectually* is simple enough. Yet in actuality, He made it clear that we must inwardly completely transform ourselves in order to enter the Realm of Divine Mind, where we are allowed to create any life we can imagine:

> Verily, verily, I say unto thee, except a man be born again, he cannot see the kingdom of God. [503]

What does it mean to be "born again"? Jesus answered the question in the following cabalistic manner:

> Verily I say unto you, except ye be converted, and become as little children, ye shall not enter into the kingdom of heaven. [504]

What did He mean by this, and why is "becoming as little children" vital to entering the Kingdom of God?

THE CHILDLIKE MIND

The short answer is that a rigid restricted mind does not allow spiritual growth, while a flexible open mind does, and the desire to grow spiritually is one of the main reasons we leave our paradisiacal home in Heaven to come here to Earth School.

Thus Jesus said we must psychologically restore our minds to that of a child, [505] or what Zen Buddhists call "beginner's mind." For a child's mind is much like our Higher Self, our Divine Self, our Indwelling Christ, [506] Luke's the "Holy One," [507] the Hindus' "Paramatma": it is naturally pure, selfless, open, guilt-free, flexible, guileless, humble, loving, trusting, and enthusiastic. Why? Because children have not yet been mentally sullied by worldly society, by atheistic science, or by dogmatic manmade religion.

False human-invented notions like shortage, famine, illness, poverty, and warfare, are incomprehensible to children. They see only good and think only good. Furthermore, they are so innocent to the ways of the adult world with all of its fabricated preconceived ideas, that they are completely lacking any kind of mental limitations. The word "impossible" does not yet exist in their vocabulary. Being newly arrived from Heaven, where anything is possible through thought alone, a child simply *knows* that whatever he believes is fact. He has not yet been taught otherwise by his parents, school, church, or society.

This is why there is no such thing as "pretend" to a child. To a youngster, playing make-believe is actually playing real-believe, for whatever he thinks is real or is told is real, is real to him. Mass mind has not yet imbued his Conscious Mind with any sense of mental restriction; nor has it saturated it with the herd mentality, with group-think, with politics, or religion. The untainted child is a true individualist, a born freethinker, always deciding what is best for himself independently and without self-limitation; always learning and growing without placing any psychic regulations on himself.

A child is indeed a natural "disciple" of God, and in the purest definition of the word: "pupil," "student," "learner."

This is precisely why Jesus referred to His followers, not as Christians (a disparaging title first appended to them by the Pagans at Antioch),[508] but as "disciples."[509] For one cannot truly follow in Jesus' footsteps without being an eternal student; that is, without having the open, inquisitive, ever expanding mind of "a little child," without which entrance into the Inner Kingdom is barred.[510] The Lord makes these comments in The Aquarian Gospel:

> Now Jesus heard the twelve [Apostles] dispute among themselves. The spirit of the carnal self [Ego] was moving in their hearts, and they were questioning among themselves who was the greatest in the sight of God and man. And Jesus said, "You men, for shame! the greatest is the servant of the rest."
> And then he called to him a little child; he took it in his arms and said, "The greatest is the little child, and if you would be great at all you must become as is this child in innocence, in truth, in purity in life. Great men scorn not the little things of earth; he who regards and honors such a child, regards and honors me, and he who scorns a child, scorn[s] me. *If you would enter through the kingdom gate you must be humble as this little child.*
> "Hear me, you men, this child, as every other child, has one to plead its cause before the throne of God. You scorn it at your peril, men, for lo, I say, its counterpart beholds the face of God at every moment, every day. And hear me once again, he who shall cause a little one to stumble and to fall is marked, accursed; and it were better far if he had drowned himself."[511]

THE ADULT MIND

Now let us contrast the childlike mind with the adult mind, which is much more likely to operate at the level of the Lower Self, the false self, the Hindus' "Jivatma," which Paul called the "outward man,"[512] and which the Apostle John mystically referred to as "the beast that was, and is not, and yet is."[513] Having been exposed to decades of low consciousness thought, the adult mind tends to be spiritually contaminated, selfish, closed, inflexible, guileful, unloving, mistrusting, and cynical. A mind like this is severely limited, and therefore cannot think beyond what it has been taught by the mass mind.

The adult mind laughs at games of make-believe, scoffs at anything that cannot be experienced by the five senses. It firmly embraces such false ideas as shortage, famine, illness, crime, privation, and warfare. It easily succumbs to the herd mentality, and likes nothing better than to form cliques, groups, societies, organizations, political bodies, and religions with like-minded people. In the adult world independent thinking is discouraged and individualism is often regarded with something between mild bemusement and outright fear and disdain.

Which do you think is more likely to gain entrance into the Kingdom of God: one possessing the child's mind or one possessing the adult mind?

THE IMPORTANCE OF BEING CHILDLIKE

The former is spiritual life, the latter is spiritual death; so the answer is obvious: the open childlike mind allows God to work with us; the closed adult mind forces God to work against us. Our mind, in fact, is like a garden hose: it functions most efficiently when it is open and free-flowing, the equivalent of a childlike mind. But bend the hose and put a kink in it, and you have blocked the movement of the water, the equivalent of the jaded adult mind.

This is precisely why Peter asked his followers to cast off their adult minds and psychologically replace them with that of infants:

> Wherefore laying aside all malice, and all guile, and hypocrisies, and envies, and all evil speakings, *as newborn babes*, desire the sincere milk of the word, that ye may grow thereby: if so be ye have tasted that the Lord is gracious.[514]

The early Christians who wrote the outstanding Gnostic document, The Thunder: Perfect Mind, made a similar if more esoteric statement: "Advance into childhood," they proclaimed![515]

Because the Kingdom of God is a holy place of complete purity,[516] it is easy to understand why Jesus said we must regain the spiritual mind and conscience of a child before we can enter: a child's mind is completely lacking in the "impurities" of the average adult mind and conscience, for "to Spirit everything is clean."[517] This is what Paul meant when he said:

> Unto the pure all things are pure: but unto them that are defiled and unbelieving is nothing pure; but even their mind and conscience is defiled.[518]

THE KEY TO THE KINGDOM: THE PURE LIFE

In The Aquarian Gospel Jesus put it this way: Abraham Consciousness, Moses Consciousness, Cosmic Consciousness, Buddha Consciousness, Chrishna Consciousness, Christ Consciousness, or "the Mind of Christ,"[519] whatever name we choose to give it,

> sleeps in every soul, and cannot be awakened till the Holy Breath [Holy Spirit] becomes a welcome guest. This Holy Breath knocks at the door of every soul, but cannot enter in until the will of man throws wide the door. There is no power in intellect to turn the key; philosophy and science both have toiled to get a glimpse behind the veil; but they have failed. *The secret spring that throws ajar the door of soul is touched by nothing else than purity in life, by prayer and holy thought.*[520]

It is only the childlike mind, in both children and adults, that can create the "purity in life" that Jesus speaks of. And this is not difficult, as many complain. To the contrary, Jesus, speaking as the Universal Indwelling Christ, said:

> Take my *yoke* upon you, and learn of me; for I am meek and lowly in heart: and ye shall find rest unto your souls. For my *yoke* is easy, and my burden is light.[521]

The biblical English word yoke derives from the Greek word *zeugos*, which is also spelled yoga, for both words mean the same thing: "balance" or "union." Thus Jesus is actually saying "my yoga is easy."[522]

In other words, it is nearly effortless to find atonement (at-one-ment) with our Real Self, our Divine Nature, THE CHRIST, "in whose spirit," as in a child, "there is no guile."[523]

Attaining union with the Mind of Christ,[524] "beginner's mind," the childlike mind, is so important that our Lord gave us these admonitions in the Gospel of Matthew:

> And Jesus called a little child unto him, and set him in the midst of them, and said, "Verily I say unto you, except ye be converted, and become as little children, ye shall not enter into the kingdom of heaven. Whosoever therefore shall humble himself as this little child, the same is greatest in the kingdom of heaven.
>
> "And whoso shall receive one such little child in my name receiveth me. But whoso shall offend one of these little ones which believe in me, it were better for him that a millstone were hanged about his neck, and that he were drowned in the depth of the sea. . . . Take heed that ye despise not one of these little ones; for I say unto you, that in heaven their angels [spiritual helpers] do always behold the face of my Father [Divine Mind] which is in heaven.
>
> "For the Son of man is come to save that which was lost. How think ye? if a man have an hundred sheep, and one of them be gone astray, doth he not leave the ninety and nine, and goeth into the mountains, and seeketh that which is gone astray? And if so be that he find it, verily I say unto you, he rejoiceth more of that sheep, than of the ninety and nine which went not astray. Even so it is not the will of your Father which is in heaven, that one of these little ones should perish."[525]

JESUS WANTS US TO BE FREETHINKING INDIVIDUALS

The childlike mind is also inherently individualistic, an extremely important attribute, for as we have seen, the group-oriented adult mind is not allowed entrance into the Kingdom of God. The "gate" is only wide enough to allow one person through at a time, eliminating "membership" to organizations, cults, sects, denominations, and religions altogether. Thus, only those individuals who have cast off the herd mentality and learned to think and make decisions for themselves are granted access to the Kingdom Within.[526]

A middle man is not needed for us to connect to God. In fact, the Father prefers direct one-on-one communication with us. This is, after all, why He made the "Way" to His Kingdom difficult and the "gate" at the entrance narrow![527]

Why is individualism so vital to Jesus' teaching on the Law of Attraction?

God does not dwell within groups of people, organizations, or religions. He dwells within individuals. Thus, in order to copartner with each one of us on the physical plane,[528] He has to individuate Himself into each one of us. This makes each human being divine in his or her our own right, a personal and unique expression or individualization of the Almighty; the literal embodiment of the Supreme Being on earth, "the Word made flesh."[529] This is why Paul said, "it is God which worketh in you both to will and to do of his good pleasure,"[530] and it is why Jesus quoted the Old Testament, saying: "You are gods."[531]

THE ONE UNFORGIVABLE SIN

This means that speaking out against our individuality, our uniqueness, or anyone else's, is speaking out against our divinity, our Godship, our Christship, the Indwelling Savior, the very life spark that vivifies us,[532] and which gives us access to the Divine Mind (the Father).[533]

Another name for our Divine Nature[534] is the Holy Ghost, or "Comforter Within."[535] Here is what Jesus said about denying the third member of the Godhead:

> Wherefore I say unto you, all manner of sin and blasphemy shall be forgiven unto men: but the blasphemy against the Holy Ghost shall not be forgiven unto men. And whosoever speaketh a word against the Son of man, it shall be forgiven him: but whosoever speaketh against the Holy Ghost, it shall not be forgiven him, neither in this world, neither in the world to come.[536]

Jesus is unambiguous: those who blaspheme against Him will be exempted,[537] but those who blaspheme against the Holy Ghost will be held accountable. Jesus placed our inner Divine Nature[538] higher up on the spiritual scale than Himself!

HONOR YOUR TRUE SELF

What is the inner meaning of these scriptures? Jesus (the Son of Man) represents the Conscious Mind ("Master"), the mind of the group. The Holy Ghost (Holy Spirit) represents the Subconscious Mind ("Servant"), the mind of the individual. It is a forgivable sin to disrespect the

Conscious Mind, for merely being the *mortal* aspect of man's brain, its sole spiritual task is to think. But to disrespect the Subconscious Mind is unforgivable, for the Subconscious Mind is the *eternal* aspect of man's brain, whose sole spiritual task is to create using its inborn divine powers!

The Subconscious is, in other words, part of our Divine Nature, our God-Self, the very essence of the Creator, the Father, individualized in us.[539] Because of this, if we dishonor it in anyway through wrong-thinking, by way of the unbending Law of Reciprocity or Law of Attraction, we only draw more of the same into our lives. Hence, Jesus' warning.

The moral? Respect your individuality, as well as the individuality of others. Ignore the negative thinking trends of the mass mind, for those who follow it "like sheep have gone astray."[540] Instead, learn to think for yourself. This is true godlike behavior!

ONLY THE SOLITARY CAN ENTER THE KINGDOM

Thinking for yourself illuminates the world because you are operating from your real self, THE CHRIST, which is in us all.[541] Just as importantly, the freethinker honors his divinity, respecting the true God Within.[542] This is the authentic meaning of the phrase "fear the Lord"[543] or "fear God"[544] (fear being used here in the Medieval English sense of "respect" or "honor").

Jesus had this to say about the importance of being a freethinking nonconformist like Himself:

> If any man come to me, and hate not his father, and mother, and wife, and children, and brethren, and sisters, yea, and his own life also, he cannot be my disciple.[545]

The inner meaning:

> If one wants to enter the Kingdom Within, he must be willing to think entirely for himself, even ignoring the social and religious beliefs of his entire family and all of his relations; even going as far as rejecting his own Ego desires; otherwise he will never achieve oneness with the Indwelling Christ.[546]

In The Gospel of Thomas, Jesus phrases this concept more starkly:

> There are many people standing outside the door of the Kingdom. But *only the solitary will be allowed to enter the chamber of enlightenment.*[547]

WE MUST "WORK OUT OUR OWN SALVATION"

There are no clear cut systematized instructions in the Bible for how an adult is to recover the individualistic mind of a child—and for good reason. We must work it out for ourselves, for it is one of the great psychological "mysteries of the Kingdom of God" that Jesus taught.[548] In other words, it is a deeply spiritual, intuitive process that cannot be learned via sermons, books, or by any other external means. From our human perspective here on earth, hidden by the God-imposed veil that separates us from Heaven, we truly "see through a glass, darkly."[549]

Yet, we know this much: since we possess an Inner Divinity,[550] and since the Kingdom is within us,[551] the solution to the riddle must be found within us as well, through self-revealed knowledge or Gnosis—that is, intuition (being self-taught, from within) as opposed to tuition (being taught by someone else, from without)[552]—as some of the first Christians called it.[553] Paul referred to Gnosis as that which "passeth [outer] knowledge."[554]

St. John of the Cross left us this piece of advice: "The soul must lose entirely its human knowledge and human feelings, in order to receive Divine knowledge and Divine feelings," and this can only come through our intuition (our sixth sense), and through wholly immersing ourselves in God. Thus, the 13th-Century Benedictine nun, Saint Mechthild of Hackeborn, said: "My soul swims in the Godhead like a fish in water!" According to William R. Inge, the saint "believed that, in answer to her prayers, God had so united Himself with her that she saw with His eyes, and heard with His ears, and spoke with His mouth."[555]

It is from this form of personal revelation, this direct knowledge or Gnosis, the inner "Divine Library," the "Invisible College," that both Jesus[556] and Paul[557] attained their wisdom, and it is why Paul said that you must "work out your own salvation."[558] For God made it impossible for us to understand Him, know Him, or become one with Him based on either group knowledge or our own limited human knowledge.[559] Thus in The Gospel of Thomas Jesus says: "If you accept and acknowledge that which is *within you*, it will bring you salvation."[560]

Remember: while *religion* is an *outer* group-oriented experience, *spirituality* is an *inner* individual-oriented one.[561] Paul, one of the earliest mystical Christians, said:

> But let every man prove his own [spiritual] work, and then shall he have rejoicing *in himself alone*, and not in another.[562]

HOW TO BE "BORN AGAIN"

The ever enigmatic Jesus left us but one sibylline clue about how to be "reborn." Let us look once more at the following passage, focusing on the word "again":

> Verily, verily, I say unto thee, except a man be born *again*, he cannot see the kingdom of God.[563]

The original Greek word here is *anothen*, which is traditionally translated as "again." But another meaning for *anothen* is "anew," so the sentence could also read:

> Verily, verily, I say unto thee, except a man be born anew [mentally], he cannot enter the Realm of Divine Mind.[564]

This provides a psychological sense, getting us closer to the truth.

The most accurate translation of *anothen*, however, is "from above, from a higher place." The sentence would then read:

> Verily, verily, I say unto thee, except a man be born from above, he cannot enter the Realm of Divine Mind.[565]

The phrase "from above" is an arcane Christian reference to the Higher Self, the immortal preexistent Indwelling Christ[566] that lived before Jesus.[567] It is the "true Light,"[568] the "hidden man of the heart,"[569] the "Ancient of Days,"[570] the "inner man,"[571] the "inward man,"[572] "the Living One who is now amongst you,"[573] symbolized in Hinduism by the Crown Chakra (Paul called it the "incorruptible crown,"[574] Peter called it the "crown of glory"),[575] which lies within every one of us, and which makes our word flesh;[576] that is, manifests our desires in the physical.[577]

So Jesus is saying that our inner transformation toward becoming more mentally childlike can be achieved by focusing on the Christ Presence Within, the Great I AM.[578]

IMITATING JESUS

The most advantageous way of doing this is by imitating Jesus, "for the kingdom of God is not meat and drink; but righteousness, and peace, and joy in the Holy Ghost."[579] And this is done through righteous living, righteous thought, righteous words, and righteous action. This would include prayer,[580] affirmations,[581] meditation,[582] fasting,[583] studying the Word of God (any sacred scripture),[584] and intoning or chanting the holy names of God,[585] along with developing such Christlike characteristics as unconditional love,[586] charitableness,[587] nonviolence,[588] tolerance,[589] and generosity[590] toward others.[591] This is spirituality, not religiosity!

Whatsoever ye do unto others, ye do unto yourself.[592] Thus being philanthropic, for instance, causes others to be philanthropic toward you. And so Jesus said that "it is more blessed to give than to receive."[593] This is just one example out of thousands illustrating how we can access the Inner Kingdom by harnessing our divine powers to work for us instead of against us.

In short, by following Jesus' commandments, "ye are complete in Him";[594] that is, you become in tune with your real self, your God-Self, while achieving atonement (at-one-ment) with the Universal Mind, which has its earthly counterpart in the mind of a child. As our consciousness rises to the level of the Divine Child Within, we make ourselves suitable to "enter the Kingdom of God,"[595] which in turn makes it easier and more fulfilling to create the Divine Life on earth that was promised us.

WHY JESUS EMPHASIZED THE KINGDOM

Now you know why Jesus placed so much significance on entering the Kingdom of God, why He preached almost nothing else: He wants us to be happy and live the most fulfilling lives we can. Now you know why He mentions the word "salvation" only once in the entire New Testament (and then not in relation to Himself);[596] why He never mentions "atonement"; why His enlightened followers preached the doctrine of Universal Salvation;[597] and why the phrase "original sin" is missing from the Bible altogether.[598]

You now know why the word "kingdom" appears 150 times in the New Testament and why nearly all of Jesus' parables are about the Kingdom of God. Most importantly, now you know why, unlike His posthumous followers, Jesus preached "the Gospel of the Kingdom"[599] rather than "the Gospel of Jesus Christ,"[600] a teaching so intriguing, so holy, so mystifying, that even "the angels desire to look into it"![601]

THE CHRISTLIKE LIFE IS OUR SALVATION

In the end, the salvific experience of enlightenment, that is, "entering into the Kingdom," will come from exactly what Jesus preached: your realization that you are a god, with powers equal to or even greater than His; supernatural abilities that enable you to create the here and now bliss[602] that our Lord called "the Kingdom of Heaven Within."[603]

How do you become God-realized in order to gain entrance into the Kingdom? First you must spiritualize yourself through the transforming experience of Christ Consciousness, Paul's "Mind of Christ,"[604] which comes from learning to think spiritually (intuitively) rather than religiously (rationally). This awakening is the first key to the Kingdom, for it allows you to understand the hidden meaning behind Jesus' esoteric teachings.

Now with your Christ Mind, read the following words, uttered by Jesus as the Universal Indwelling Christ:

> I am the door: by me if any man enter in, he shall be saved, and shall go in and out, and find pasture.[605]

"The door" the Master speaks of here is not a real door. It is a mystical one; that is, a psychological door. It is, in fact, the veritable entrance to the Kingdom of God within us, and it unlatches and swings open with the second key: following Jesus' commandments.[606] How does one do this?

In simplest terms we must imitate Him by doing precisely what He did: accept our innate Godhood,[607] our Divine Nature,[608] and strive to be Christlike. This means being loving,[609] compassionate,[610] merciful,[611] tolerant,[612] and forgiving.[613]

And this is surely something anyone can do, for not only do both the Father[614] and the Holy Ghost exist within us,[615] but THE CHRIST—"the true Light which lighteth every man that cometh into the world"[616]—does as well.[617] For just as Paul said: *"Christ is all and in all"!*[618]

In Nobis Regnat Christus

Notes

1. See Eusebius, *History of the Church*, 3:39.

2. For Paul's reference, see Acts 20:35, where he cites a saying by Jesus that is not found in the canonical Bible.

3. In the minds of the Q people, once Q was absorbed into Matthew, Luke, and Mark (not to mention numerous other noncanonical Gospels and works), they probably saw little reason to preserve it. Thus, it gradually fell out of use and eventually vanished. After all, it was considered a theological document, not a historical one. At the time then, little or no importance was attached to it. Examples of the Gospel of Q that were used in the Gospel of Matthew: 5:3-4, 6, 39, 42, 44-47; 6:9-13; 7:7-11, 12; 10:26-31, 39; 8:20-22; 16:25.

4. At least 35 percent of the words in The Gospel of Thomas parallel those in Q.

5. The Gospel of Thomas (and its 114 sayings, or doctrines of Jesus) was discovered at Nag Hammadi, Egypt, in 1945, with the first English translation coming out in 1959. This particular (physical) document has been dated to around the year A.D. 340, although earlier corroborating finds at Oxyrhynchus, Egypt, date back to at least A.D. 130. Due to the style, wording, and tone of The Gospel of Thomas, the Nag Hammadi and Oxyrhynchus fragments must have been based on a scroll containing the core sayings of Jesus that was composed as early as the 30s or 40s A.D., that is, the Gospel of Q. Thus, the original Gospel of Thomas was probably written sometime between A.D. 50 and 75. This makes The Gospel of Thomas—which may actually turn out to be a version of the Gospel of Q— of particular importance to those who are interested in learning about the pre-Christian, pre-Paganized, pre-politicized, pre-Catholicized figure of Jesus, His original teachings, and His original followers, the Jesus community of Q.

6. Acts 10:34.

7. See e.g., Matthew 19:12.

8. Hebrews 4:12.

9. John 1:5.

10. Colossians 3:1; Romans 8:11.

11. See e.g., The Book of Thomas the Contender, Logion 1, and The Gospel of Thomas, Introduction and Logion 1.

12. See e.g., Matthew 4:23; 9:35; Mark 1:14.

13. For more on this fascinating topic see Seabrook, JLOA, Appendix B.

14. Pike, pp. 599-600.

15. John 5:30-31; 12:44-45.

16. John 14:24.

17. John 14:20.

18. John 14:16-17; 1 Corinthians 6:19; 2 Corinthians 1:22; 2 Timothy 1:14.

19. John 10:30; 17:22; 1 Corinthians 6:17; 12:12; 2 Corinthians 6:16; Ephesians 4:6.

20. John 10:34.

21. Genesis 1:16-27.

22. Galatians 1:16.

23. Colossians 3:11.

24. The Gospel of Thomas, Logion 1. My paraphrasal.

25. See The Secret Book of James, 7:8-14.

26. Genesis 2:7. See also 1 Corinthians 15:45.

27. No human language contains words that can properly depict the Soul. Personally I like the description given by Hindu scripture, which says that the soul is "one ten-thousandth the size of a point," a meaningless dimension that cannot be measured by modern science. See Prabhupada, p. 57.

28. Whiston, Vol. 3, p. 437.

29. Genesis 1:26-27.

30. Pike, p. 252.

31. Inge, p. 359. "This spark was created with the soul in all men, and is a clear light in them, and strives in every way against sin, and impels steadily to virtue, and presses ever back to the source from which it sprang." Inge, p. 360.

32. John 10:34.

33. John 16:24.

34. Pike, p. 239.

35. John 14:12. In the Gnostic Christian work The Secret Book of James (also known as The Apocryphon of James), 6:17-20, Jesus tells His Twelve Apostles: "Become better than I; make yourselves like the son of the Holy Spirit."

36. Pike, p. 518.

37. Genesis 3:22.

38. Psalms 82:6.

39. Isaiah 41:23.

40. See e.g., John 17:21; Hebrews 12:10; 2 Peter 1:4.

41. See e.g., Mark 3:21; John 10:19-20.

42. See e.g., Matthew 26:65-66; Mark 14:64; John 10:24-39. Mainstream Christianity teaches that Jesus died to fulfill Old Testament prophecies concerning the Messiah. Historically, however, it has been proven that this belief did not emerge until long after His death and resurrection; in other words, it was a fabrication of the 4th-Century Catholic Church. Is this particular Christian dogma then true or not? I will leave it to the reader to decide. But first let us consider the words of our Lord Himself: "O fools, and slow of heart to believe all that the prophets have spoken" (Luke 24:25).

43. John 10:34.

44. John 10:22-40.

45. Pertaining to John 10:34: here the KJV has long used the singular Greek word theos (θεος), meaning a "god" or "God" (the singular Greek word for "goddess" is thea). Taking theos then, if we translate Jesus' statement literally, He is actually saying: "you are god," or even "you are God." This meaning, of course, correlates exactly with the metaphysical teachings of mystical Christianity, that we are not just merely gods and goddesses in our own right, but, being extensions or individualizations of the Divine, we are each a piece of God the Father Himself. Thus, the esoteric (inner) meaning of "you are gods" is "you are God." It is intriguing to note that the scripture Jesus is quoting, Psalms 82:6, uses the Hebrew word elohim, which, depending on various factors, can be either plural, meaning "gods" or "goddesses," or plural intensive-singular, meaning "god" or "goddess," or also "God." Additionally we will note that the earliest (currently) known Greek word used in John 10:34 is the plural word theoi (θεοι), meaning "gods" (the plural Greek for "goddesses" is theai). If the original and complete Gospel of John is ever found, it will be of great scholarly and theological interest to see what word was actually used in this particular scripture: theoi ("gods") or theos "god"). Mystically, however, it will make little difference, for both words have the same spiritual meaning and significance.

46. John 17:20-23.

47. Galatians 4:7.

48. Galatians 4:19.

49. Colossians 3:10-11.

50. See e.g., Acts 17:7, where both Caesar and Jesus are referred to as a "king." In Acts 26:28, during his conversation with Paul, King Herod Agrippa uses the word "Christian" derogatorily, for as a royal he has been christed ("anointed") and is therefore already a "Christ." Emperor Julius Caesar was called "God manifest and Universal Savior of the human race," while Emperor Augustus was known as "Our hereditary God and Savior of all humanity."

51. See e.g., Leviticus 4:3; 1 Samuel 2:10; 2 Samuel 1:21; 1 Chronicles 16:22; Psalms 18:50; Isaiah 45:1; Lamentations 4:20; Daniel 9:25-26; Habakkuk 3:13.

52. See e.g., Matthew 1:1, 18. Contrary to popular thought "Christ" is an honorific title, not Jesus' last name.

53. See e.g., Matthew 16:16-17, 20; Mark 8:29-30; Luke 9:20-21; 22:67; John 1:41; 11:27; 20:31; 1 John 2:22; 5:1.

54. 2 Corinthians 13:5.

55. Colossians 1:27. See also Romans 8:10; 1 Corinthians 6:15, 17; 2 Corinthians 5:16; 13:3, 5.

56. Philippians 2:5.

57. John 1:26.

58. Philippians 2:6.

59. Genesis 1:26-27.

60. John 1:9.

61. Daniel 7:13-14.

62. Hebrews 1:3.

63. John 10:34; 14:20.

64. See the Gnostic Christian work, The Prayer of the Apostle Paul. See also Deuteronomy 10:17; Psalms 136:3; 1 Timothy 6:15; Revelation 17:14; 19:16.

65. Matthew 16:16-17, 20; Mark 8:29-30; Luke 9:20-21; 22:67; John 1:41; 11:27; 20:31; 1 John 2:22; 5:1.

66. Matthew 22:41-46. See also Matthew 28:20.

67. John 8:58.

68. Revelation 22:13.

69. John 6:62.

70. John 17:5.

71. John 17:24.

72. According to His own words, Jesus did not intend to overturn the old religion (Judaism), nor did He intend to create a new faith in His name—not Christianity or any other religion. See e.g., Matthew 5:17. Rather, as the Sermon on the Mount patently illustrates, the Lord's intention was to initiate a return to a more mystical form of spirituality, one free of the pseudorighteousness, dogmatic formalism, pathological creeds, empty ceremonialism, censorious diatribes, and imperious fundamentalism of the religious Pharisees, militaristic Herodians, and political Sadducees, whom Jesus is shown repeatedly cursing, damning, and vilifying. Seabrook, JLOA, p. 423.

73. For more on this topic, see Seabrook, JLOA, Appendix b.

74. Hebrews 13:8.

75. My paraphrasal.

76. Inge, p. 77.

77. Eusebius, *History of the Church*, 2:17. See also Crusé, p. 68.

78. The Tripartite Tractate, 3:34-35. My paraphrasal.

79. 1 Corinthians 10:1-4.

80. Ephesians 1:4-5. See also Philippians 2:13.

81. Colossians 1:15-17.

82. 1 Peter 1:20.

83. Daniel 7:14.

84. Proverbs 26:10.

85. Genesis 1:26-27.

86. 2 Peter 1:4.

87. Hebrews 12:10.

88. Colossians 3:11.

89. Micah 5:2.

90. Proverbs 20:27.

91. Revelation 1:16.

92. Malachi 4:2.

93. See e.g., The Gospel of Thomas, Logion 24.

94. As I point out in my book *Christmas Before Christianity* (pp. 68, 77), Jesus' title, Christ, derives from the old Babylonian word for the Chaldean sun-god, *Chris*; in Hebrew, *hrs*, or with vowels, *heres*. The Greeks later borrowed *Chris* for their word for anointing, *christos*, which became Christ, "the anointed," in English.

95. Baigent, Leigh, and Lincoln, p. 367.

96. Seabrook, JLOA, p. 438.

97. Revelation 5:5.

98. John 8:12.

99. Cuthbert, p. 421.

100. John 12:36.

101. Ephesians 5:14.

102. My paraphrasal.

103. Colossians 1:25-27.

104. My paraphrasal.

105. Romans 6:4-5.

106. Romans 8:11.

107. Colossians 3:1-4.

108. Philippians 2:5-6.

109. My paraphrasal.

110. 1 Timothy 6:16.

111. 1 John 3:2.

112. 1 John 3:1.

113. Gaskell, s.v. "Son of God"; "Son of Man."
114. See e.g., Genesis 1:26-27; 3:22. See *Strong's Exhaustive Concordance of the Bible*, word number 0430.
115. Exodus 6:3; Psalms 83:18; Isaiah 12:2; 26:4. See *Strong's Exhaustive Concordance of the Bible*, word number 03068.
116. Fillmore, s.v. "Jehovah."
117. Romans 8:14.
118. Genesis 1:27.
119. Galatians 4:3-7. See also Romans 8:15.
120. The Acts of Paul and Thecla, 1:19. My paraphrasal.
121. Levi, 92:11-12.
122. Matthew 1:1.
123. John 1:12.
124. Psalms 45:7.
125. Galatians 2:20; 2 Corinthians 13:5.
126. 2 Corinthians 1:21.
127. 1 Corinthians 15:28.
128. Due to their close comparison in the book of Hebrews (7:3, 21), some early Christian mystery schools taught that Jesus was a reincarnation of Melchizedek, as did the ancient Gnostic Christians. See e.g., the Gnostic Christian Jewish document entitled, Melchizedek. My mainstream Christian copy of the King James Bible lists Melchizedek as a "type of Christ." See also Psalms 110:4; Revelation 22:13. We will note here that the doctrine of reincarnation was both accepted and taught by Jesus and the Apostles (see e.g., Matthew 3:1-2; 11:11-15; 14: 1-2; 16:13-14; 17:10-13; 26:52; Mark 6:14-15; 8:27-28; 9:11-13; Luke 9:7-8, 18-19; John 1:19-21, 25; 3:3-13; 8:56-58; 9:1-3; 14:1-3, 12; Romans 9:10-14; Ephesians 1:4; Hebrews 2:2-3; Revelation 3:12), as well as many of the Church Fathers, such as Origen, Saint Jerome, and Clement of Alexandria. Reincarnation was branded a "heresy" at the Second Council of Constantinople in 553, and banned from Church teachings.
129. Hebrews 7:3. Hindus preach the same doctrine: all who attain at-one-ment with God (Christhood) become a Melchizedek or Christ. Thus the enlightened ancient Hindu teacher and philosopher Sri Adi Shankara wrote: "Mind, nor intellect, nor ego, feeling . . . I am He, I am He, Blessed Spirit, I am He! No birth, no death, no caste have I; Father, mother, have I none. . . ."
130. Daniel 7:13-14.
131. Besides Jesus and Melchizedek, many other enlightened souls have been described in this manner. One modern example is the great Indian Saint Sri Mahavatar Babaji, who is known as the "deathless sage." The miracle-working holy man, who has "no birthday, parents, or family," is at least hundreds of years old, a fact attested to by the many individuals who have encountered him over the centuries. Despite this, the "ageless and immortal" Babaji, who, like Jesus, can levitate, biolocate, perform instant healings, and raise the dead (among many other "miracles"), is said to still be walking the earth to this day, usually—though he can take on any physical form—appearing to startled eyewitnesses as a radiant young man. It is believed that he lives secretly in the Himalayas. See Yogananda, *AOAY*, pp. 353, 360, 402-403.
132. Matthew 16:16-17, 20; Mark 8:29-30; Luke 9:20-21; 22:67; John 1:41; 11:27; 20:31; 1 John 2:22; 5:1.
133. Jeremiah 31:33.
134. Matthew 24:14. See also Matthew 4:23; 9:35; Luke 4:43.
135. Yogananda, TSCOC, Vol. 1, p. 6.
136. Revelation 14:6.
137. The word gospel derives from the Old English words *gōd* ("good") and *spell* ("tale").
138. 1 Corinthians 11:7.
139. Ephesians 4:13.
140. Fillmore, s.v. "Jehovah."
141. Genesis 1:26-27.
142. See John 10:34; 14:20.
143. 2 Corinthians 1:21.
144. 2 Corinthians 11:10.
145. Galatians 1:16.
146. 1 John 5:10.
147. 1 John 5:20. See also 1 John 2:5.
148. 1 John 2:20.
149. Galatians 4:19.

150. 2 Corinthians 4:4.

151. Genesis 1:26-27.

152. See e.g., The Secret Gospel of James, 10:5.

153. 2 Corinthians 3:18.

154. See e.g., Yogananda, WFE, pp. 66-67.

155. Matthew 24:23.

156. Daniel 7:13-14.

157. John 12:32; 14:20; 15:4; 17:21-23, 26; Colossians 1:27; 3:10-11; Romans 8:10; 1 Corinthians 6:15, 17; 2 Corinthians 5:16; 13:3, 5; Galatians 1:16; 2:20; 4:19; Ephesians 3:14-17; Philippians 1:20; 2:5; 1 Peter 1:11; 1 John 2:27; 3:24; 4:4.

158. John 14:8-11.

159. See Isaiah 64:8.

160. 2 Corinthians 4:7.

161. 2 Corinthians 4:11.

162. Galatians 3:25.

163. 1 John 2:27.

164. Matthew 23:10. See also Colossians 4:1; 2 Corinthians 13:5.

165. Matthew 7:7; Luke 11:9.

166. Spiritual knowledge can only be gained spiritually, not intellectually. See 1 Corinthians 1:17-31; 2:1-16.

167. Psalms 8:5. Here, the KJV uses the word "angel," a seemingly purposeful mistranslation of the original *elohim*, a Hebrew masculine word whose traditional meaning is usually defined as "a plurality of male deities," but is usually written, misleadingly, as simply "God." In some mystical Christian schools, however, the Elohim is a group of seven female deities, the daughters of the enigmatic priest Melchizedek. In others the Elohim is comprised of seven pairs of male and female couples: 1) Hercules and Amazonia, 2) Apollo and Lumina, 3) Heros and Amora, 4) Astrea and Purity, 5) Cyclopea and Virginia, 6) Peace and Aloha, and 7) Arcturus and Victoria. In the Bible the Elohim are known occultly as "the seven spirits of God" (see e.g., Revelation 3:1; 4:5; 5:6) and the "morning stars" that "sang together" (Job 38:7). In traditional mainstream Christianity the Elohim are the creators of the Universe, Man, and all life on earth, as the Bible itself attests. While the first chapter of Genesis mistranslates the plural elohim as the singular "God," the device is given away in verse 26: "And God said, 'Let *us* make man in *our* image, after *our* likeness.'" (Note: the feminine singular of elohim is *eloah*, "goddess," which derives from the divine name-title, El, the name of the Canaanite Supreme male god and father of Baal. The name-title El was absorbed by the ancient Hebrews, becoming a generic name for God. See e.g., Psalms 18:31; 33, 48; 68:21; Job 8:3. El is also used by the Old Testament writers as a prefix fronting other various names of God. See e.g., Genesis 14:18; 17:1; Joshua 3:10. Sometimes the biblical Father is referred to as "El, the God [Elohim]," as in Genesis 33:20.)

168. 1 Corinthians 6:3.

169. Luke 20:36.

170. Graham, *Angels*, passim.

171. Jeremiah 23:6; 33:16.

172. John 17:21; Hebrews 12:10; 2 Peter 1:4.

173. Colossians 1:27.

174. 1 Corinthians 6:15, 17; 2 Corinthians 5:16; 13:3, 5.

175. Daniel 7:13-14.

176. Romans 6:6; Galatians 2:20.

177. Colossians 3:1-3.

178. Galatians 1:16. My paraphrasal.

179. Daniel 7:13-14.

180. Matthew 22:41-46. See also Daniel 7:13-14; Micah 5:2; Matthew 28:20; John 8:58; Hebrews 7:3; Revelation 22:13.

181. Psalms 46:10.

182. Exodus 3:14.

183. Exodus 6:3; Psalms 83:18; Isaiah 12:2; 26:4. See *Strong's Exhaustive Concordance of the Bible*, word number 03068.

184. See e.g., Matthew 16:16-17, 20; Mark 8:29-30; Luke 9:20-21; 22:67; John 1:41; 11:27; 20:31; 1 John 2:22; 5:1.

185. John 17:21; Hebrews 12:10; 2 Peter 1:4.

186. Exodus 3:4.

187. 1 Corinthians 15:10.

188. Galatians 4:12.

189. Just as Christians teach that Jesus is the Logos or the Word, Hindus teach that God is the Aum or Om, the "Creative Word."

190. The name Solomon (Sol-Om-On), meaning the "Sun-God of On," indicates that he was an ancient Hebrew rendition of the archetypal sun-god, known in Egypt as Ra, in Greece as Apollo, in Persia as Mitra or Mithra (later Mithras), and in Mesopotamia as Shamash (Chemosh of the Bible). See e.g., 1 Kings 11:7, 33. Thus mystically Solomon and his 1,000 "wives, princesses, and concubines" (1 Kings 11:3) symbolize the Solar System, with the women representing the planets and various other celestial bodies. Solomon's "black" lover (see e.g., Song of Solomon 1:1-4, 5-8) is none other than the Egyptian Isis, Supreme Mother-Goddess and personification of the earth (that is, black topsoil).

191. Revelation 1:8, 11; 21:6.

192. Revelation 3:14. For John's corresponding Gospel text, see John 1:1-3.

193. Revelation 22:13.

194. Hebrews 3:4.

195. 2 Corinthians 3:18.

196. Pike, p. 380.

197. Isaiah 40:6.

198. Galatians 4:19.

199. Colossians 3:11.

200. Genesis 1:27.

201. Matthew 5:48.

202. Ephesians 3:16.

203. Romans 7:22.

204. 1 Peter 3:4.

205. Acts 3:14.

206. Daniel 7:9, 13, 22.

207. Hebrews 13:8.

208. John 12:34.

209. John 12:32; 14:20; 15:4; 17:21-23, 26; Colossians 1:27; 3:10-11; Romans 8:10; 1 Corinthians 6:15, 17; 2 Corinthians 5:16; 13:3, 5; Galatians 1:16; 2:20; 4:19; Ephesians 3:14-17; Philippians 1:20; 2:5; 1 Peter 1:11; 1 John 2:27; 3:24; 4:4.

210. John 18:5-6.

211. Mark 14:61-62.

212. John 8:23.

213. John 6:35.

214. John 10:7. In Hinduism, this cosmic "door" is viewed as a spiritual portal through which trained yogis can leave and reenter their physical bodies at will. Thus Jesus, speaking as the Indwelling Christ, said: " I am the door: by me if any man enter in, he shall be saved, and shall go in and out, and find pasture." John 10:9.

215. John 10:11.

216. John 8:12.

217. Revelation 1:18.

218. John 13:13.

219. Matthew 11:29.

220. John 18:37.

221. John 14:6.

222. John 15:1.

223. Mark 14:61-62.

224. Matthew 13:55; Mark 6:3; Luke 3:23; 4:22; John 1:45; 6:42; Galatians 4:4. See also Seabrook, JATGOQ, passim. According to a recently discovered text known as the "Slavonic Josephus" (which is probably a copy of the original unedited version of the great historian's works), Jesus was an ordinary man. See Baigent, Leigh, and Lincoln, pp. 377-378; Eisler, pp. 167, 427.

225. Romans 1:3. Many later Christian sects also claimed that Jesus was a mortal human being, among them were the 3rd-Century Manichaeans, the 4th-Century Arians, the Medieval Cathars, and the 18th-Century Camisards. Baigent, Leigh, and Lincoln, pp. 384-385, 431.

226. Mark 1:10. In traditional Christianity Jesus was the Son of God from birth. In mystical Christianity, however, He adopted this title only after His baptism in the Holy Spirit. The New Testament itself bears witness to this fact. The celebrated Lucan scripture, "Thou art my beloved Son; in thee I am well pleased" (Luke 3:22), is missing from our earliest known New Testament manuscripts, such as the Codex Bezae (written perhaps about the year 400). In its place we find the following passage, which is no doubt the original: "Thou art my Son; today I have begotten thee." Thus, according to the earliest Gospel writers, Jesus only became a Son of God (God-realized) at the time of His baptism. This is supported in turn by another fact: as the Gospel of Q (the earliest written collection of Jesus' teachings) shows, the historical Jesus referred to Himself not as the "Son of God," but as the "Son of Man" (meaning a human being). The former phrase then could only have been appended to His biblical biography by the Church (priesthood) after His death, just as Acts 8:37 (in which Jesus is called the "Son of God") reveals: this passage is an obvious interpolation, for it is not found in the earliest known New Testament texts (such as the Codex Sinaiticus). For more on this topic, see Seabrook, JLOA, pp. 399-400, 407-409.

227. Daniel 7:13-14.

228. Colossians 3:11.

229. The Gospel of Thomas, Logion 77. My paraphrasal. Jesus probably patterned this secret teaching on Ecclesiastes 10:9.

230. See Mark 14:63-64.

231. Acts 24:14.

232. John 1:14.

233. Matthew 22:41-46. See also Daniel 7:13-14; Micah 5:2; Matthew 28:20; John 8:58; Colossians 1:17; Hebrews 7:3; Revelation 22:13.

234. John 8:58.

235. Genesis 11:26.

236. Genesis 17:5.

237. Ephesians 4:6.

238. John 8:23-24; 27-28.

239. My paraphrasal.

240. Daniel 7:13-14.

241. Genesis 17:1; Exodus 3:14-15; Psalms 46:10; Mark 8:29; 14:61-62; Luke 22:70; John 6:35; 8:12, 23, 58; 9:5; 10:7-11, 30-39; 11:25; 12:26, 46; 13:13; 14:3, 6, 10-11, 20; 15:1; 17:10, 16.

242. John 13:19.

243. Colossians 1:19; 2:9.

244. John 10:30. Zen Buddhists have a similar saying. *Namu Dai Butsu*: "I am one with the great Buddha."

245. John 17:23; Galatians 3:28.

246. Colossians 1:27.

247. Ephesians 2:6, 13.

248. John 17:11.

249. John 17:21-22.

250. See e.g., Isaiah 9:6; Matthew 22:41-45; John 1:1; 14:9; 1 Timothy 3:16; Titus 1:3. Indeed, many mainstream Christian churches today teach that the Jehovah of the Old Testament "became" the man known as Jesus in the New Testament, and even translate the name of Jesus (meaning "Jehovah the Savior") as "He is Jehovah the Savior."

251. Romans 3:29-30.

252. Deuteronomy 6:4; Mark 12:29. See also Levi, 96:3-7.

253. Malachi 2:10.

254. 1 Corinthians 8:6.

255. Ephesians 4:6.

256. Seabrook, JLOA, p. 36.

257. Isaiah 42:8.

258. Romans 9:26; 2 Corinthians 6:16.

259. John 12:32; 14:20; 15:4; 17:21-23, 26; Colossians 1:27; 3:10-11; Romans 8:10; 1 Corinthians 6:15, 17; 2 Corinthians 5:16; 13:3, 5; Galatians 1:16; 2:20; 4:19; Ephesians 3:14-17; Philippians 1:20; 2:5; 1 Peter 1:11; 1 John 2:27; 3:24; 4:4.

260. Colossians 1:15-17.

261. John 1:1-14. See also John 8:58; Psalms 90:2; 1 Timothy 1:17; Colossians 1:17; Hebrews 9:14; Matthew 22:41-46; Mark 12:35-37; The Gospel of Thomas, Logion 106.

262. Matthew 18:20.
263. Matthew 28:20.
264. Matthew 25:40.
265. Psalms 82:6.
266. John 10:34.
267. Romans 8:14. See also John 1:12; 1 John 3:1-2.
268. Galatians 3:28.
269. Genesis 1:26-27; 3:5, 22.
270. See Pike, p. 690.
271. Malachi 4:2.
272. Pike, p. 533.
273. John 14:9.
274. My paraphrasal.
275. Philippians 3:8.
276. Hebrews 12:10.
277. Leviticus 11:44-45.
278. Psalms 86:2.
279. The doctrine of the hypostatic union—as pertaining only to Jesus—is a late creation of the Catholic Church, which did not formally adopt the concept until the 6th Century, at the Fifth General Council of Constantinople held in A.D. 533. Before that Christians held a myriad of different beliefs on the subject. Among them were those forwarded by such doctrinal authorities as Eutyches, Arius, Apollinaris, and Nestorius.
280. Colossians 2:9-10.
281. Galatians 3:20.
282. Luke 20:36; Romans 8:16.
283. See Genesis 17:1; Exodus 3:14-15; Psalms 46:10; Mark 8:29; 14:61-62; Luke 22:70; John 6:35; 8:12, 23, 58; 9:5; 10:7-11, 30-39; 11:25; 12:26, 46; 13:13; 14:3, 6, 10-11, 20; 15:1; 17:10, 16.
284. Romans 12:5.
285. John 14:20.
286. Fox, p. 103.
287. Leadbeater, pp. 47-48.
288. *Refutation of All Heresies*, Book 10, Chapter 30.
289. *City of God*, Book 11, Chapter 26.
290. Gaskell, s.v. "Birth of Jesus."
291. Angus, p. 106.
292. Inge, p. 359.
293. Inge, p. 362.
294. Theosophical Society, p. 182.
295. Keble, pp. 281-282, 225, 449, 550.
296. From a letter to Adelphos.
297. Robertson, pp. 83-84.
298. John 10:34.
299. Clement is also the originator of the famous phrase: "The human soul is training itself to be God." See Inge, p. 357.
300. Angus, p. 106. My paraphrasal.
301. John 10:34.
302. From Clement's *The Stromata*, Book 1, Chapter 10.
303. Inge, p. 357.
304. *Summa Theologica*, Part 3, Question 16, Article 7.
305. *Summa Theologica*, Part 1, Question 15, Article 2. My paraphrasal.
306. *Summa Theologica*, Part 2, Question 45, Article 6.
307. Romans 8:28-30.
308. Fox, pp. 110-111, 116-118.
309. Johnson, p. 293.
310. See e.g., Prabhupada, p. 131.
311. Inge, p. 156.
312. Julian of Norwich, p. 15.

313. Inge, p. 321.

314. Acts 17:28. Paul is quoting the noted Greek poet Aratus of Cilicia, who lived in the 4th and 3rd Centuries B.C. A crater on our moon was named after Aratus.

315. Yogananda, WFE, p. 30.

316. Baba, p. 17. My paraphrasal.

317. From the poem, *Song of Myself.*

318. I have paraphrased John 17:10.

319. Romans 8:16-17.

320. John 10:34.

321. See my book, *Jesus and the Gospel of Q: Christ's Pre-Christian Teachings As Recorded in the New Testament.*

322. See e.g., Matthew 13:55; Mark 6:3; Luke 3:23; 4:22; John 1:45; 6:42.

323. Mark 14:61-62.

324. Seabrook, JLOA, pp. 399-400, 407-409.

325. John 14:20.

326. 1 John 4:8; 16.

327. Levi, p. 9.

328. Levi, 178:45-46.

329. Levi, 68:13-14.

330. Matthew 11:15.

331. Matthew 13:46.

332. John 12:32; 14:20; 15:4; 17:21-23, 26; Colossians 1:27; 3:10-11; Romans 8:10; 1 Corinthians 6:15, 17; 2 Corinthians 5:16; 13:3, 5; Galatians 1:16; 2:20; 4:19; Ephesians 3:14-17; Philippians 1:20; 2:5; 1 Peter 1:11; 1 John 2:27; 3:24; 4:4.

333. Hebrews 5:5-6; 6:20. See also Hebrews 7:3. We believers are all members of a very special spiritual community, "a royal priesthood," as Peter called it. 1 Peter 2:9.

334. Levi, 15:22; Hebrews 9:24.

335. Hebrews 8:2. My paraphrasal. See also Hebrews 9:11; Baba, p. 44.

336. Matthew 22:41-46. See also Daniel 7:13-14; Micah 5:2; Matthew 28:20; John 8:58; Colossians 1:17; Hebrews 7:3; Revelation 22:13.

337. Exodus 3:14; Ezekiel 37:14; John 14:10-11; Romans 8:9, 11; 1 Corinthians 3:16; 6:17; 14:25; 2 Corinthians 6:16; 9:14; Ephesians 2:22; 4:6; Philemon 2:13; 1 John 3:24; 4:4, 12-13, 16; Zechariah 2:10.

338. Levi, 163:37.

339. Luke 10:16.

340. John 12:45.

341. John 14:20.

342. John 10:34.

343. 2 Corinthians 3:18.

344. 2 Corinthians 1:21.

345. Genesis 1:27.

346. See John 1:18.

347. Colossians 1:15.

348. 1 John 4:12. See also John 1:18.

349. John 10:38; 14:8-13.

350. 1 Corinthians 2:16.

351. The "First Coming" occurs when we are born and our soul, THE CHRIST, is implanted in a physical body. Thus, ancient Gnostic Christians, as they continue to do today, taught the doctrine of "spiritual resurrection" (the spirit leaves the body and ascends into Heaven) as opposed to "physical resurrection" (the spirit and the body remain intact and ascend into Heaven together). For more on the Gnostic Christian view of resurrection see the following works: The Treatise on the Resurrection, The Gospel of Philip, The Testimony of Truth, The Exegesis On the Soul, and The Gospel of Thomas. Some of the canonical works also contain Gnostic elements regarding the resurrection. See e.g., 1 Corinthians 15:50; Romans 6:5; 2 Timothy 2:18; 1 John 2:28; John 11:25.

352. Mark 13:32.

353. Daniel 7:13-14.

354. Colossians 2:9.

355. John 12:32; 14:20; 15:4; 17:21-23, 26; Colossians 1:27; 3:10-11; Romans 8:10; 1 Corinthians 6:15, 17; 2 Corinthians 5:16; 13:3, 5; Galatians 1:16; 2:20; 4:19; Ephesians 3:14-17; Philippians 1:20; 2:5; 1 Peter 1:11; 1 John 2:27; 3:24; 4:4.

356. John 14:23.

357. Colossians 2:10.

358. Philippians 2:5-6.

359. John 1:12; Romans 8:14, 19; Philippians 2:15; 1 John 3:2.

360. For more on the topics of achieving perfect health, spiritual healing, and the divine curing of disease, see Seabrook, JLOA, pp. 283-350.

361. Job 22:28.

362. 1 Corinthians 6:17; 2 Corinthians 6:16, 18; Ephesians 4:6. See also 2 Samuel 7:14; 1 Chronicles 17:13; Isaiah 43:6; Jeremiah 31:9.

363. Levi, 91:35-36, 38-41.

364. Romans 13:1.

365. Deuteronomy 6:4; Isaiah 42:8; Mark 12:29.

366. See Levi, 8:2.

367. Romans 11:36.

368. Matthew 22:32.

369. John 14:20.

370. The Epistle of Paul to the Laodiceans, 1:11.

371. Hebrews 12:10.

372. 2 Peter 1:4.

373. See John 10:34; 14:12.

374. John 15:5.

375. Dr. Sagan's original statement was: "The cosmos is also within us. We're made of star stuff. We are a way for the cosmos to know itself." Powerful and wonderful words from one of the world's greatest skeptical scientists.

376. From Emerson's essay, "Compensation."

377. Romans 8:16-17.

378. Colossians 3:24.

379. See e.g., Matthew 19:24.

380. Seabrook, JLOA, p. 397.

381. John 18:36.

382. Luke 17:21. Also see The Gospel of Thomas, Logion 3.

383. My paraphrasal.

384. Matthew 10:7.

385. See e.g., Matthew 5:3, 10.

386. The Gospel of Thomas, Logion 51. My paraphrasal.

387. See e.g., Matthew 12:28.

388. Luke 17:21.

389. Luke 16:16.

390. See e.g., Matthew 5:20; 7:21; 18:3; 19:23-24.

391. See Seabrook, JLOA, pp. 76-81.

392. John 14:20.

393. John 10:34. See also Psalms 82:6.

394. John 10:38; 14:8-13.

395. Inge, p. 358.

396. 1 Peter 4:1.

397. Matthew 22:9.

398. Matthew 8:11.

399. 1 Thessalonians 2:12.

400. 1 Peter 5:7.

401. Psalms 91:1, 10.

402. Psalms 23:1-6.

403. 2 Timothy 1:7.

404. Matthew 6:25-33.

405. John 12:32; 14:20; 15:4; 17:21-23, 26; Colossians 1:27; 3:10-11; Romans 8:10; 1 Corinthians 6:15, 17; 2 Corinthians 5:16; 13:3, 5; Galatians 1:16; 2:20; 4:19; Ephesians 3:14-17; Philippians 1:20; 2:5; 1 Peter 1:11; 1 John 2:27; 3:24; 4:4.
406. Matthew 19:28; Luke 22:30; 2 Timothy 2:12; Revelation 3:12, 21; 5:10; 20:6; 22:5.
407. Luke 17:20-21.
408. Mark 11:24.
409. For more on this topic, see Seabrook JLOA, passim; BLOA, passim.
410. Matthew 24:14. See also Matthew 4:23; 9:35; Luke 4:43.
411. Mark 1:1.
412. John 7:16.
413. Mark 9:41; John 17:3.
414. John 8:28-29, 40, 42, 50, 54.
415. John 12:26.
416. See e.g., Psalms 2:4-12; Exodus 12:15; 15:3; 34:14; 35:2-3; Numbers 11:32-36; 31:1-18; Deuteronomy 2:30-34; 3:6; 7:1-6; 18:20; 20:16-17; 22:20-21; Leviticus 21:9; 24:16; Joshua 6:17-21; 7:10-26; 8:26; 10:28-40; 11:10-21; Judges 18:6, 27; 1 Samuel 6:19; 15:1-8, 33; 18:27; 2 Samuel 8:4; 1 Chronicles 21:1-15; 1 Kings 18:40; 2 Kings 19:35. There are numerous other biblical scriptures illustrating the unpredictable barbarity of the Paganized Old Testament "Lord of Lords," the Pagan-styled Hebrew sky-god that Jesus did away with. See e.g., Lamentations 2:21; 3:10-11; Hosea 13:7-8; Ezekiel 6:12-13; 8:17-18; Isaiah 13:6-18; Micah 6:9-16; Nahum 1:2-6; Habakkuk 3:5; Zephaniah 1:2-3.
417. Seabrook, JLOA, pp. 94, 253.
418. Proverbs 23:7.
419. Matthew 3:2; 4:17; 5:3, 10; 10:7.
420. Matthew 19:26; Revelation 3:8.
421. 2 Peter 1:10-11.
422. 1 Corinthians 1:4-5.
423. Levi, 71:3-7.
424. Matthew 22:14.
425. Matthew 7:21-23.
426. Matthew 8:11.
427. Matthew 21:31.
428. Acts 14:22.
429. 2 Thessalonians 1:5.
430. The Sermon on the Mount, for example (which Jesus partially patterned on a group of exhortatory scriptures known as the Testaments of the Twelve Patriarchs—fragments of which were recently found among the Dead Sea Scrolls), is essentially the Master's entire teaching on the Kingdom of God, which includes, for example, many of His Law of Attraction doctrines. See Matthew 5:1-48; 6:1-34; 7:1-29.
431. Genesis 17:1; Exodus 3:14-15; Psalms 46:10; Mark 8:29; 14:61-62; Luke 22:70; John 6:35; 8:12, 23, 58; 9:5; 10:7-11, 30-39; 11:25; 12:26, 46; 13:13; 14:3, 6, 10-11, 20; 15:1; 17:10, 16.
432. Galatians 2:20.
433. Galatians 5:24.
434. Mark 8:35.
435. John 12:32; 14:20; 15:4; 17:21-23, 26; Colossians 1:27; 3:10-11; Romans 8:10; 1 Corinthians 6:15, 17; 2 Corinthians 5:16; 13:3, 5; Galatians 1:16; 2:20; 4:19; Ephesians 3:14-17; Philippians 1:20; 2:5; 1 Peter 1:11; 1 John 2:27; 3:24; 4:4.
436. Ecclesiastes 12:8.
437. 2 Peter 1:5-11.
438. 1 Corinthians 2:16.
439. Daniel 7:13-14.
440. Psalms 27:1.
441. Hebrews 12:2.
442. Galatians 5:24.
443. See Colossians 2:13-14. Here Paul refers to the Lower Self as the "flesh" and the Higher Self as the "Christ."
444. Galatians 2:20.
445. Philippians 1:21.
446. My paraphrasal.

447. Romans 6:6; Ephesians 4:22; Colossians 3:9.
448. Ephesians 2:15; 4:24; Colossians 3:10.
449. Romans 12:2.
450. 1 John 2:13.
451. Colossians 3:1-3.
452. Isaiah 55:6-8.
453. Matthew 6:22-23.
454. Luke 9:23.
455. The Epistle of Barnabas, 10:11.
456. Whittick, p. 226.
457. Biedermann, s.v. "Cross."
458. Walker, pp. 46-64.
459. Cirlot, s.v. "Cross."
460. King James' scribes translated "Holy of Holies" as "most holy place." See e.g., Exodus 26:34; Numbers 18:10; 2 Chronicles 4:22.
461. See e.g., Ezekiel 41:4.
462. See e.g., Romans 2:6-7.
463. This is the same reason hypnosis must be repeated periodically on individuals seeking to rid their minds of negative beliefs, ideas, and concepts.
464. For more on this ancient well established principle, see my books: *Jesus and the Law of Attraction* and *The Bible and the Law of Attraction.*
465. Enlightened Hindus rightly call death, that is, the shedding of the physical body, "kicking the frame."
466. Ephesians 2:18; Romans 5:1-2; 8:10; 1 Corinthians 6:15, 17; 2 Corinthians 5:16; 13:3, 5.
467. Romans 6:23.
468. My paraphrasal.
469. See 2 Corinthians 4:16.
470. Romans 7:18-25.
471. 1 Peter 5:8.
472. 1 Corinthians 15:31.
473. Romans 8:36.
474. 2 Corinthians 4:16.
475. Ephesians 4:22-24.
476. Genesis 1:26-27.
477. Matthew 10:32-40.
478. Matthew 11:12.
479. Matthew 9:16-17.
480. My paraphrasal.
481. Levi, 120:8-11.
482. 1 Corinthians 2:9; 2 Epistle of Clement, 4:14.
483. Matthew 26:29.
484. Romans 12:2.
485. Luke 20:25.
486. John 10:34.
487. John 14:12.
488. See e.g., Mark 3:21; John 10:20.
489. See e.g., Matthew 5:1; 14:23; Mark 1:12-13, 35; 6:46-47; Luke 4:1; 5:15-16; 6:12; John 6:15.
490. Matthew 7:13-14. Pre-Christian religions have long taught this same spiritual concept. The Katha Upanishad of the Hindus, for instance, possesses this scripture: "Like the sharp edge of a razor, the sages say, is the path. Narrow it is, and difficult to tread."
491. My paraphrasal.
492. Matthew 5:3, 10.
493. Matthew 21:31.
494. Matthew 19:30.
495. Galatians 5:20-21.
496. See e.g., 1 Corinthians 1:17-31; 2:1-16.
497. Luke 17:21.

498. 1 Timothy 1:17.

499. Matthew 10:16.

500. Luke 13:18-21.

501. Matthew 6:33.

502. Luke 18:29-30.

503. John 3:3.

504. Matthew 18:3.

505. Matthew 18:3.

506. John 12:32; 14:20; 15:4; 17:21-23, 26; Colossians 1:27; 3:10-11; Romans 8:10; 1 Corinthians 6:15, 17; 2 Corinthians 5:16; 13:3, 5; Galatians 1:16; 2:20; 4:19; Ephesians 3:14-17; Philippians 1:20; 2:5; 1 Peter 1:11; 1 John 2:27; 3:24; 4:4.

507. Acts 3:14.

508. Acts 11:26. See Seabrook, JLOA, Appendix B.

509. See e.g., Matthew 12:49; Mark 6:1; Luke 6:13; John 4:1.

510. Mark 10:15.

511. Levi, 131:8-15.

512. 2 Corinthians 4:16.

513. Revelation 17:8.

514. 1 Peter 2:1-3.

515. My paraphrasal.

516. Romans 14:17.

517. Levi, 126:24.

518. Titus 1:15.

519. 1 Corinthians 2:16.

520. Levi, 44:22-25.

521. Matthew 11:29-30.

522. Seabrook, JLOA, p. 114.

523. Psalms 32:2.

524. 1 Corinthians 2:16.

525. Matthew 18:1-6; 10-14.

526. Ephesians 2:18; Romans 5:1-2; 8:10; 1 Corinthians 6:15, 17; 2 Corinthians 5:16; 13:3, 5.

527. Matthew 7:14.

528. Psalms 30:10; 1 Corinthians 3:9; 2 Corinthians 6:1; Ephesians 2:19-22; Hebrews 13:6.

529. John 1:14.

530. Philippians 2:13.

531. John 10:34. See also Genesis 1:27; Psalms 82:6; Isaiah 41:23.

532. Colossians 1:27; Romans 8:10.

533. Ephesians 2:18; Romans 5:1-2; 8:10; 1 Corinthians 6:15, 17; 2 Corinthians 5:16; 13:3, 5.

534. John 17:21; Hebrews 12:10; 2 Peter 1:4.

535. See e.g., John 14:16-17. See also John 14:26.

536. Matthew 12:31-32.

537. This is particularly true for those who blaspheme due to ignorance in spiritual unbelief. See e.g., 1 Timothy 1:13.

538. John 17:21; Hebrews 12:10; 2 Peter 1:4.

539. John 17:21; Hebrews 12:10; 2 Peter 1:4.

540. Isaiah 53:6.

541. Colossians 3:11.

542. Exodus 3:14; Ezekiel 37:14; John 14:10-11; Romans 8:9, 11; 1 Corinthians 3:16; 6:17; 14:25; 2 Corinthians 6:16; 9:14; Ephesians 2:22; 4:6; Philemon 2:13; 1 John 3:24; 4:4, 12-13, 16; Zechariah 2:10.

543. See e.g., Deuteronomy 6:13; Psalms 115:11, 13.

544. Ecclesiastes 12:13; 1 Peter 2:17; Revelation 14:7.

545. Luke 14:26.

546. My paraphrasal.

547. The Gospel of Thomas, Logion 75. My paraphrasal.

548. Luke 8:10. See also Matthew 13:11.

549. 1 Corinthians 13:12.

550. John 10:34.

551. Luke 17:21.

552. The Secret Book of James, 1:12.

553. Early Christians, both Gnostic and Ecclesiastic, taught that we cannot know God through the intellect, only through the "heart" (that is, intuition, our "sixth sense"). As such, as Jesus taught, knowledge of God must come from within, from "my Father which is in heaven," not from without. See e.g., Matthew 16:17. See also Luke 2:26; 10:21; 1 Corinthians 1:17-31; 2:1-16; Galatians 1:11-12; Ephesians 3:1-5; 1 Peter 1:12.

554. Ephesians 3:19.

555. Inge, p. 365.

556. See e.g., John 7:14-17.

557. Galatians 1:11-12.

558. Philippians 2:12. See also Levi, 100:17. Buddha made a similar comment: "Work out your salvation with diligence."

559. 1 Corinthians 1:17-31; 2:1-16. Thus, one enlightened soul, Socrates, once said: "As for me, all I know is that I know nothing."

560. The Gospel of Thomas, Logion 70. My paraphrasal.

561. See Romans 2:28-29.

562. Galatians 6:4.

563. John 3:3.

564. My paraphrasal.

565. My paraphrasal.

566. John 12:32; 14:20; 15:4; 17:21-23, 26; Colossians 1:27; 3:10-11; Romans 8:10; 1 Corinthians 6:15, 17; 2 Corinthians 5:16; 13:3, 5; Galatians 1:16; 2:20; 4:19; Ephesians 3:14-17; Philippians 1:20; 2:5; 1 Peter 1:11; 1 John 2:27; 3:24; 4:4.

567. Matthew 22:41-46. See also Daniel 7:13-14; Micah 5:2; Matthew 28:20; John 8:58; Hebrews 7:3; Revelation 22:13.

568. John 1:9.

569. 1 Peter 3:4.

570. Daniel 7:9, 13, 22.

571. Ephesians 3:16.

572. Romans 7:22.

573. The Gospel of Thomas, Logion 52. My paraphrasal.

574. 1 Corinthians 9:25. Early Christians also referred to the Crown Chakra (a symbol of spiritual enlightenment) as the "Crown of Rejoicing" (1 Thessalonians 2:19), "Crown of Righteousness" (2 Timothy 4:8), "Crown of Life" (James 1:12; Revelation 2:10; Levi, 95:17), "Crown of Glory" (1 Peter 5:4), and the "Golden Crown" (Revelation 14:14). The New Testament portrays the Virgin Mary "clothed with the sun," wearing a similar coronate symbol: a "crown of twelve stars" (Revelation 12:1), an obvious borrowing from the much older Hindu sun-goddess Aditi, who wore a crown of twelve stars representing the twelve signs of the Zodiac.

575. 1 Peter 5:4.

576. John 1:14.

577. Luke 11:2.

578. Genesis 17:1; Exodus 3:14-15; Psalms 46:10; Mark 8:29; 14:61-62; Luke 22:70; John 6:35; 8:12, 23, 58; 9:5; 10:7-11, 30-39; 11:25; 12:26, 46; 13:13; 14:3, 6, 10-11, 20; 15:1; 17:10, 16.

579. Romans 14:17.

580. See e.g., Acts 6:4; Ephesians 6:18; Colossians 4:2.

581. See e.g., Titus 3:8.

582. See e.g., Psalms 5:1; 19:14; 49:3; 104:34; 119:97, 99.

583. See e.g., Acts 14:23; 1 Corinthians 7:5.

584. See e.g., 2 Timothy 3:14-17.

585. See e.g., Exodus 15:1; Judges 5:3; 2 Samuel 22:50; 1 Chronicles 15:28; 16:7-11, 23-25; 2 Chronicles 20:18-21; 29:25-30; Isaiah 12:4-5; Psalms 57:7-11; 98:4-6; 146:1.

586. See e.g., Jeremiah 31:3; Luke 6:27; Romans 12:9-10; 1 Corinthians 13:1-13; 1 John 4:7-11, 16-18.

587. See e.g., 1 Corinthians 13:4, 8, 13.

588. See e.g., Matthew 5:21-22; 18:3; 22:40; 38-41; 43-46; Luke 6:27-38; John 14:22.

589. See e.g., John 8:7; Acts 10:28; Ephesians 4:2; Romans 14:1-4; 1 Peter 3:8-11.

590. See e.g., Psalms 37:26; Proverbs 11:24-25; 19:17; Luke 6:38; 12:33; Acts 20:35; 2 Corinthians 9:6.

591. Some 500 years before Christ, Buddha laid out his own eight-part guideline for attaining Self-Godhood. It is known as the Noble Eightfold Path: 1) Right View; 2) Right Intention; 3) Right Speech; 4) Right Action; 5) Right Livelihood; 6) Right Effort; 7) Right Mindfulness; and 8) Right Concentration. As all of the world's most enlightened individuals tap into the same universal consciousness, it is probable, or at least possible, that Jesus' eight Beatitudes are loosely based on Buddha's eight "Beatitudes." See Matthew 5:3-10.

592. Matthew 7:12.

593. Acts 20:35.

594. Colossians 2:10.

595. Matthew 5:20; 7:21; 18:3; 19:23-24.

596. Luke 19:9.

597. Luke 3:6; Romans 10:13; Acts 2:17; 2 Peter 3:9.

598. For more on these topics, see Seabrook, JLOA, Appendix A and Appendix B.

599. Matthew 24:14. Jesus publicly uttered this phrase one or two years *before* His death, sometime in A.D. 32 or 33. See also Luke 4:43.

600. Mark 1:1. This passage was written about the year A.D. 60, some twenty-seven years (a generation) *after* Jesus' death. See Seabrook, JLOA, Appendix B.

601. 1 Peter 1:12.

602. Romans 14:17.

603. Luke 17:21.

604. 1 Corinthians 2:16.

605. John 10:9.

606. John 14:15.

607. John 10:34.

608. 2 Peter 1:4.

609. Matthew 22:35-40.

610. Matthew 9:36; 14:14; 15:32; 20:34; Mark 1:41; 5:19; 6:34; 8:2; Luke 7:13.

611. Matthew 9:13; Luke 1:50, 54, 58.

612. John 8:1-11.

613. Matthew 6:14; Mark 11:25; Luke 17:4.

614. John 10:30; 17:22; 1 Corinthians 6:17; 12:12; 2 Corinthians 6:16; Ephesians 4:6.

615. John 14:16-17; 1 Corinthians 6:19; 2 Corinthians 1:22; 2 Timothy 1:14.

616. John 1:9.

617. John 12:32; 14:20; 15:4; 17:21-23, 26; Colossians 1:27; Romans 8:10; 1 Corinthians 6:15, 17; 2 Corinthians 5:16; 13:3, 5; Galatians 1:16; 2:20; 4:19; Ephesians 3:14-17; Philippians 1:20; 2:5; 1 Peter 1:11; 1 John 2:27; 3:24; 4:4.

618. Colossians 3:11.

"Neither pray I for these alone, but for them also which shall believe on me through their word; *that they all may be one; as thou, Father, art in me, and I in thee, that they also may be one in us:* that the world may believe that thou hast sent me. And *the glory which thou gavest me I have given them; that they may be one, even as we are one: I in them, and thou in me, that they may be made perfect in one;* and that the world may know that thou hast sent me, and hast loved them, as thou hast loved me." — The Indwelling Christ (John 17:20-23)

Bibliography

And Suggested Reading

Abbott, Walter, Rabbi Arthur Gilbert, Rolfe Lanier Hunt, and J. Carter Swaim (eds.). *The Bible Reader: An Interfaith Interpretation.* London, UK: Geoffrey Chapman, 1969.

Anderson, J. N. D. *Christianity and Comparative Religion.* 1970. Downers Grove, IL: InterVarsity Press, 1974 ed.

Andrews, Ted. *The Occult Christ: Angelic Mysteries, Seasonal Rituals, and the Divine Feminine.* St. Paul, MN: Llewellyn, 1993.

Angus, Samuel. *The Mystery-Religions and Christianity: A Study of the Religious Background of Early Christianity.* 1925. New York, NY: Citadel Press, 1966 ed.

Baba, Meher. *Life At Its Best.* 1957. New York, NY: E. P. Dutton, 1976 ed.

Baigent, Michael, Richard Leigh, and Henry Lincoln. *Holy Blood, Holy Grail.* 1982. New York, NY: Dell, 1983 ed.

Banton, Michael (ed.). *Anthropological Approaches to the Study of Religion.* 1966. London, UK: Tavistock, 1973 ed.

Barnstone, Willis (ed.). *The Other Bible.* San Francisco, CA: Harper and Row, 1984.

Bauval, Robert, and Adrian Gilbert. *The Orion Mystery: Unlocking the Secrets of the Pyramids.* New York, NY: Crown, 1994.

Biedermann, Hans. *Dictionary of Symbolism: Cultural Icons and the Meanings Behind Them.* 1989. New York, NY: Facts On File, 1992 ed.

Boardman, John, Jasper Griffin, and Oswyn Murray. *The Roman World.* 1986. Oxford, UK: Oxford University Press, 1988 ed.

Bucke, Richard Maurice. *Cosmic Consciousness: A Study in the Evolution of the Human Mind.* 1901. Philadelphia, PA: Innes and Sons, 1905 ed.

Bulfinch, Thomas. *Bulfinch's Mythology: The Age of Fable, the Age of Chivalry, Legends of Charlemagne.* New York, NY: Grosset and Dunlap, 1913.

Burtt, Edwin A. (ed.). *The Teachings of the Compassionate Buddha.* New York, Mentor, 1955.

Butler, Trent C. (ed.). *Holman Bible Dictionary.* Nashville, TN: Holman, 1991.

Campbell, Joseph. *The Hero With a Thousand Faces.* 1949. Princeton, NJ: Princeton University Press, 1973 ed.

——. *Transformations of Myth Through Time.* New York, NY: Harper and Row, 1990.

Christie-Murray, David. *A History of Heresy.* 1976. Oxford, UK: Oxford University Press, 1990 ed.

Cirlot, J. E. *A Dictionary of Symbols.* 1962. New York, NY: Philosophical Library, 1983 ed.

Cooper, J. C. *Symbolic and Mythological Animals.* Hammersmith, UK: The Aquarian Press, 1992.

Cotterell, Arthur. *The Macmillan Illustrated Encyclopedia of Myths and Legends.* New York, NY: Macmillan, 1989.

Courtenay, William J. (ed.). *The Judeo-Christian Heritage.* New York, NY: Holt, Rinehart and Winston, 1970.

Cross, F. L., and E. A. Livingstone (eds.). *The Oxford Dictionary of the Christian Church.* 1957. London, UK: Oxford University Press, 1974 ed.

Crusé, Christian Frederick (trans.). *The Ecclesiastical History of Eusebius Pamphilus, Bishop of*

Cesarea, in Palestine. 1833. New York, NY: Stanford and Swords, 1850 ed.

Cumont, Franz. *The Mysteries of Mithra*. Chicago, IL: Open Court Publishing Co., 1903.

Curtiss, Harriette Augusta, and F. Homer Curtiss. *The Key to the Universe, or a Spiritual Interpretation of Numbers and Symbols*. Washington, D.C.: The Curtiss Philosophic Book Co., 1917.

Cuthbert, Father. *Life of St. Francis of Assisi*. 1912. London, UK: Longmans, Green and Co., 1914 ed.

Davies, A. Powell. *The Meaning of the Dead Sea Scrolls*. New York, NY: Mentor, 1956.

Davis, John J. *Biblical Numerology: A Basic Study of the Use of Numbers in the Bible*. 1968. Grand Rapids, MI: Baker Book House, 1988 ed.

Dowley, Tim (ed.). *The History of Christianity*. Oxford, UK: Lion, 1977.

Eisenman, Robert, and Michael Wise. *The Dead Sea Scrolls Uncovered*. Rockport, MA: Element, 1992.

Eisler, Robert. *The Messiah Jesus and John the Baptist: According to Flavius Josephus' Recently Rediscovered 'Capture of Jerusalem' and the Other Jewish and Christian Sources*. London, UK: Methuen, 1931.

Eliade, Mircea. *The Sacred and the Profane: The Nature of Religion*. 1957. San Diego, CA: Harcourt Brace Jovanovich, 1959 ed.

Eliot, Alexander. *The Universal Myths: Heroes, Gods, Tricksters and Others*. 1976. New York, NY: Meridian, 1990 ed.

Farmer, David Hugh. *The Oxford Dictionary of Saints*. 1978. Oxford, UK: Oxford University Press, 1992 ed.

Ferguson, George. *Signs and Symbols in Christian Art*. 1954. Oxford, UK: Oxford University Press, 1975 ed.

Fillmore, Charles. *Metaphysical Bible Dictionary*. Unity Village, MO: Unity School of Christianity, 1931.

Finigan, Jack. *Light From the Ancient Past: The Archaeological Background of the Hebrew-Christian Religion* (Vol. 1). 1946. Princeton, NJ: Princeton University Press, 1974 ed.

Fischer, Carl. *The Myth and Legend of Greece*. Dayton, OH: George A. Pflaum, 1968.

Fox, Matthew. *The Coming of the Cosmic Christ: The Healing of Mother Earth and the Birth of a Global Renaissance*. San Francisco, CA: Harper and Row, 1988.

Frazier, James G. *The Golden Bough: A Study of Comparative Religion*. 2 vols. London, UK: Macmillan and Co., 1890.

——. *Folklore in the Old Testament*. 3 vols. London, UK: Macmillan and Co., 1919.

Gaskell, G. A. *Dictionary of All Scripture and Myths*. 1960. New York, NY: Julian Press, 1973 ed.

Gimbutas, Marija. *The Goddesses and Gods of Old Europe: 6500-3500 BC, Myths and Cult Images*. 1974. Berkeley, CA: University of California Press, 1992 ed.

Goguel, Maurice. *Jesus and the Origins of Christianity*. 2 vols. 1932. New York, NY: Harper, 1960 ed.

Gorman, Melvin. *The Pagan Bible*. Portland, OR: Binfords and Mort, 1962.

Graham, Billy. *Angels: Ringing Assurance that We Are Not Alone*. 1975. Nashville, TN: Thomas Nelson, 1995 ed.

——. *The Holy Spirit: Activating God's Power in Your Life*. Waco, TX: Keyword, 1978.

Graves, Kersey. *The World's Sixteen Crucified Saviors; or Christianity Before Christ*. Boston, MA: Colby and Rich, 1876.

Graves, Robert, and Raphael Patai. *Hebrew Myths: The Book of Genesis*. New York, NY: Anchor, 1964.

Grimal, Pierre. *Dictionary of Classical Mythology*. 1951. Harmondsworth, UK: Penguin, 1990 ed.

Guignebert, Charles. *The Christ*. 1943. New York, NY: Citadel, 1968 ed.

Harpur, James. *The Atlas of Sacred Places: Meeting Points of Heaven and Earth*. New York, NY:

Henry Holt and Co., 1994.

Hooke, S. H. *Middle Eastern Mythology*. 1963. Harmondsworth, UK: Penguin, 1991 ed.

Inge, William Ralph. *Christian Mysticism*. London, UK: Methuen and Co., 1899.

Johnson, Henry (trans.). *The Divine Comedy of Dante Alighieri*. New Haven, CT: Yale University Press, 1915.

Jones, A. H. M. *Constantine and the Conversion of Europe*. 1948. New York, NY: Collier, 1962 ed.

Julian of Norwich. *Sixteen Revelations of Divine Love*. London, UK: R. F. S. Cressy, 1843.

Keble, John. *Five Books of S. Irenaeus: Against Heresies*. London, UK: James Parker and Co., 1872.

Kee, Howard Clark. *The Origins of Christianity: Sources and Documents*. Englewood Cliffs, NJ: Prentice-Hall, 1973.

Kelly, J. N. D. *Early Christian Doctrines*. 1960. New York, NY: Harper and Row, 1978 ed.

Küng, Hans. *Christianity: Essence, History, and Future*. New York, NY: Continuum, 1995.

Lamsa, George M. *The Holy Bible: From Ancient Eastern Manuscripts*. 1933. Philadelphia, PA: A. J. Holman, 1968 ed.

Leadbeater, Charles Webster. *Some Glimpses of Occultism: Ancient and Modern*. 1903. Chicago, IL: The Rajput Press, 1909 ed.

Levi. *The Aquarian Gospel of Jesus the Christ: The Philosophic and Practical Basis of the Religion of the Aquarian Age of the World and of the Church Universal*. Los Angeles, CA: E. S. Dowling, 1911.

Lewis, Abram Herbert. *Paganism Surviving in Christianity*. New York, NY: G. P. Putnam's Sons, 1892.

Lewis, H. Spencer. *The Secret Doctrines of Jesus*. 1937. San Jose, CA: The Rosicrucian Press, 1979 ed.

Lindsey, Hal. *The Rapture: Truth or Consequences*. New York, NY: Bantam, 1983.

Littleton, C. Scott (ed.). *Mythology: The Illustrated Anthology of World Myth and Storytelling*. London, UK: Duncan Baird, 2002.

Livingstone, Elizabeth Anne (ed.). *The Concise Oxford Dictionary of the Christian Church*. 1977. Oxford, UK: Oxford University Press, 1990 ed.

Lurker, Manfred. *The Gods and Symbols of Ancient Egypt*. 1974. London, UK: Thames and Hudson, 1984 ed.

Mack, Burton L. *The Lost Gospel: The Book of Q and Christian Origins*. San Francisco, CA: Harper Collins, 1993.

Mascaró, Juan (trans.). *The Bhagavad Gita*. Harmondsworth, UK: Penguin, 1962.

McKenzie, John L. *Dictionary of the Bible*. New York, NY: Collier, 1965.

Metford, J. C. J. *Dictionary of Christian Lore and Legend*. London, UK: Thames and Hudson, 1983.

Metzger, Bruce M., and Michael D. Coogan (eds.). *The Oxford Companion to the Bible*. New York, NY: Oxford University Press, 1993.

Meyer, Marvin W. (ed.). *The Ancient Mysteries: A Sourcebook*. San Francisco, CA: Harper and Row, 1987.

Moltmann, Jürgen. *The Crucified God: The Cross of Christ as the Foundation and Criticism of Christian Theology*. 1973. New York, NY: Harper and Row, 1974 ed.

Nee, Andrew. *The Psychology of Transcendence*. 1980. New York, NY: Dover, 1990 ed.

Neumann, Erich. *The Great Mother: An Analysis of the Archetype*. New York, NY: Pantheon, 1955.

Pagels, Elaine. *The Gnostic Gospels*. 1979. New York, NY: Vintage, 1981 ed.

Patai, Raphael. *The Hebrew Goddess*. 1967. Detroit, MI: Wayne State University Press, 1990 ed.

Paul, Pope John, II. *Crossing the Threshold of Hope*. New York, NY: Alfred A. Knopf, 1994.

Pike, Albert (ed.). *Morals and Dogmas of the Ancient and Accepted Scottish Rite of Freemasonry*.

Charleston, SC: L. H. Jenkins, 1871.

Potter, Charles Francis. *The Lost Years of Jesus Revealed.* 1958. New York, NY: Fawcett, 1962 ed.

Prabhavananda, Swami. *The Sermon on the Mount According to Vedanta.* New York, NY: Mentor, 1963.

Prabhupada, A. C. Bhaktivedanta Swami. *The Science of Self-Realization.* 1977. Los Angeles, CA: International Society for Krishna Consciousness, 1983 ed.

Preller, Victor. *Divine Science and the Science of God: A Reformation of Thomas Aquinas.* Princeton, NJ: Princeton University press, 1967.

Prophet, Mark L., and Elizabeth Clare Prophet. *The Lost Teachings of Jesus.* Livingston, MT: Summit University Press, 1986.

Richardson, Cyril C. (ed. and trans.). *Early Christian Fathers.* New York, NY: Collier, 1970.

Robertson, Archibald (trans.). *St. Athanasius on the Incarnation.* London, UK: D. Nutt, 1885.

Robertson, John M. *Christianity and Mythology.* London, UK: Watts and Co., 1900.

——. *Pagan Christs.* 1903. New York, NY: Dorset Press, 1987 ed.

Robinson, James M. (ed.). *The Nag Hammadi Library.* 1978. San Francisco, CA: Harper Collins, 1990 ed.

Schweitzer, Albert. *The Quest of the Historical Jesus: A Critical Study of Its Progress From Reimarus to Wrede.* London, UK: Adam and Charles Black, 1910.

Seabrook, Lochlainn. *The Goddess Dictionary of Words and Phrases: Introducing a New Core Vocabulary for the Women's Spirituality Movement.* 1997. Nashville, TN: Sea Raven Press, 2010 ed.

——. *The Book of Kelle: An Introduction to Goddess-Worship and the Great Celtic Mother-Goddess Kelle, Original Blessed Lady of Ireland.* 1999. Franklin, TN: Sea Raven Press, 2010 ed.

——. *Britannia Rules: Goddess-Worship in Ancient Anglo-Celtic Society - An Academic Look at the United Kingdom's Matricentric Spiritual Past.* 1999. Franklin, TN: Sea Raven Press, 2010 ed.

——. *Christmas Before Christianity: How the Birthday of the "Sun" Became the Birthday of the "Son."* Franklin, TN: Sea Raven Press, 2010.

——. *Jesus and the Law of Attraction: The Bible-Based Guide to Creating Perfect Health, Wealth, and Happiness Following Christ's Simple Formula.* Spring Hill, TN: Sea Raven Press, 2013.

——. *The Bible and the Law of Attraction: 99 Teachings of Jesus, the Apostles, and the Prophets.* Spring Hill, TN: Sea Raven Press, 2013.

——. *Jesus and the Gospel of Q: Christ's Pre-Christian Teachings As Recorded in the New Testament.* Spring Hill, TN: Sea Raven Press, 2014.

——. *Autobiography of a Non-Yogi: A Scientist's Journey From Hinduism to Christianity* (Dr. Amitava Dasgupta and Lochlainn Seabrook). Spring Hill, TN: Sea Raven Press, 2015.

——. *Seabrook's Bible Dictionary of Traditional and Mystical Christian Doctrines.* Spring Hill, TN: Sea Raven Press, 2016.

Segal, Alan F. *Paul the Convert: The Apostolate and Apostasy of Saul the Pharisee.* New Haven, CT: Yale University Press, 1990.

Shank, Hershel (ed.). *Understanding the Dead Sea Scrolls.* New York, NY: Random House, 1992.

Spalding, Baird T. *Life and Teachings of the Masters of the Far East.* 5 vols. 1924. Marina del Rey, CA: DeVorss and Co., 1964 ed.

Staniforth, Maxwell (trans.). *Early Christian Writings: The Apostolic Fathers.* 1968. Harmondsworth, UK: Penguin, 1984 ed.

Stott, John R. W. *The Cross of Christ.* Downers Grove, IL: InterVarsity Press, 1986.

Strauss, David Friedrich, Peter C. Hodgson, and George Eliot. *The Life of Jesus Critically Examined.* Philadelphia, PA: Fortress Press, 1972.

Streep, Peg. *Sanctuaries of the Goddess: The Sacred Landscapes and Objects*. Boston, MA: Bulfinch Press, 1994.

Strong, James. *Strong's Exhaustive Concordance of the Bible*. 1890. Nashville, TN: Abingdon Press, 1975 ed.

Szekely, Edmond Bordeaux. *The Essene Gospel of Peace* (Book 1). 1928. London, UK: International Biogenic Society, 1978 ed.

Theosophical Society. *The Theosophical Quarterly*, Vol. 5, No. 1, July 1907. New York, NY: The Theosophical Society, 1907.

Townsend, Rev. Mark. *Jesus Through Pagan Eyes: Bridging Neopagan Perspectives with a Progressive Vision of Christ*. Woodbury, MN: Llewellyn, 2012.

Underhill, Evelyn. *The Mystic Way: A Psychological Study in Christian Origins*. London, UK: J. M. Dent and Sons, 1913.

Wake, Archbishop (and other divines). *The Forbidden Books of the Original New Testament of Jesus Christ*. London, UK: E. Hancock and Co., 1863.

Walker, Barbara G. *The Woman's Dictionary of Symbols and Sacred Objects*. San Francisco, CA: Harper and Row, 1988.

Weigal, Arthur. *The Paganism In Our Christianity*. 1928. San Diego, CA: The Book Tree, 2008 ed.

Westcott, Frank N. *Catholic Principles*. Milwaukee, WI: The Young Churchman, 1902.

Whiston, William (trans.). *The Genuine Works of Flavius Josephus*. 3 vols. Boston, MA: Thomas and Andrews, 1809.

Whittick, Arnold. *Symbols: Signs and Their Meaning and Uses in Design*. Newton, MA: Charles T. Branford, 1971.

Yogananda, Paramahansa. *Whispers From Eternity*. 1935. Los Angeles, CA: Self-Realization Fellowship, 1973 ed.

——. *Autobiography of a Yogi*. 1946. Los Angeles, CA: Self-Realization Fellowship, 1972 ed.

——. *The Second Coming of Christ: The Resurrection of the Christ Within You*. 2 vols. Los Angeles, CA: Self-Realization Fellowship, 2004.

Young, Dudley. *Origins of the Sacred: The Ecstasies of Love and War*. 1991. New York, NY: Harper Collins, 1992 ed.

Index

NOTE: The use of an automated indexer can cause minor irregularities in entries and page numbers.

MEET THE AUTHOR

Neo-Victorian scholar Lochlainn Seabrook, a descendant of the families of Alexander Hamilton Stephens, John Singleton Mosby, Edmund Winchester Rucker, and William Giles Harding, is a 7th generation Kentuckian and the most prolific and popular pro-South writer in the world today. Known by literary critics as the "new Shelby Foote" and by his fans as the "Voice of the Traditional South," he is a recipient of the prestigious Jefferson Davis Historical Gold Medal, and, as a lifelong writer, has authored and edited books ranging in topics from history, politics, and science, to nature, religion, and the paranormal.

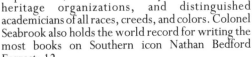

One of the world's most popular living historians, he is a 17th generation Southerner of Appalachian heritage who descends from dozens of patriotic Revolutionary War soldiers and Confederate soldiers from Kentucky, Tennessee, North Carolina, and Virginia. A proud member of the Sons of the Confederate Veterans, he is a true Renaissance Man. Besides being an accomplished and well respected author-historian and Bible authority, he is also a Kentucky Colonel, eagle scout, screenwriter, nature, wildlife, and landscape photographer, artist, graphic designer, songwriter, film composer, musician, music producer, genealogist, former history museum docent, and a former ranch hand, zookeeper, and wrangler.

His 70 adult and children's books contain some 60,000 well-researched pages that have earned him accolades from around the globe. His works, which have sold on every continent except Antarctica, have introduced hundreds of thousands to vital facts that have been left out of our mainstream books. He has been endorsed internationally by leading experts, museum curators, award-winning historians, bestselling authors, celebrities, filmmakers, noted scientists, well regarded educators, TV show hosts and producers, renowned military artists, esteemed heritage organizations, and distinguished academicians of all races, creeds, and colors. Colonel Seabrook also holds the world record for writing the most books on Southern icon Nathan Bedford Forrest: 12.

Of northern and central European descent, he is the 6th great-grandson of the Earl of Oxford and a descendant of European royalty. His modern day cousins include: Johnny Cash, Elvis Presley, Lisa Marie Presley, Billy Ray and Miley Cyrus, Patty Loveless, Tim McGraw, Lee Ann Womack, Dolly Parton, Pat Boone, Naomi, Wynonna, and Ashley Judd, Ricky Skaggs, the Sunshine Sisters, Martha Carson, Chet Atkins, Patrick J. Buchanan, Cindy Crawford, Bertram Thomas Combs (Kentucky's 50th governor), Edith Bolling (second wife of President Woodrow Wilson), Andy Griffith, Riley Keough, George C. Scott, Robert Duvall, Reese Witherspoon, Lee Marvin, Rebecca Gayheart, and Tom Cruise.

A constitutionalist and avid gun advocate, Colonel Seabrook is the author of the international blockbuster, *Everything You Were Taught About the Civil War is Wrong, Ask a Southerner!* He lives with his wife and family in beautiful historic Middle Tennessee, the heart of the Confederacy.

For more information on the author visit

LOCHLAINNSEABROOK.COM

If you enjoyed this book you will be interested in Mr. Seabrook's other popular spiritual titles:

☞ JESUS & THE LAW OF ATTRACTION: THE BIBLE-BASED GUIDE TO CREATING PERFECT HEALTH, WEALTH, & HAPPINESS
☞ JESUS & THE GOSPEL OF Q: CHRIST'S PRE-CHRISTIAN TEACHINGS AS RECORDED IN THE NEW TESTAMENT
☞ SEABROOK'S BIBLE DICTIONARY OF TRADITIONAL & MYSTICAL CHRISTIAN DOCTRINES
☞ CHRISTMAS BEFORE CHRISTIANITY: HOW THE BIRTHDAY OF THE "SUN" BECAME THE BIRTHDAY OF THE "SON"
☞ THE BOOK OF KELLE: AN INTRODUCTION TO GODDESS-WORSHIP & THE GREAT CELTIC MOTHER-GODDESS KELLE
☞ BRITANNIA RULES: GODDESS-WORSHIP IN ANCIENT ANGLO-CELTIC SOCIETY

Available from Sea Raven Press and wherever fine books are sold

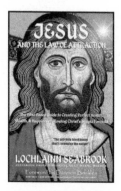

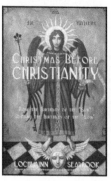

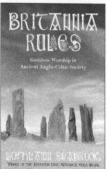

ALL OF OUR BOOK COVERS ARE AVAILABLE AS 11" X 17" POSTERS, SUITABLE FOR FRAMING.

SeaRavenPress.com

Ingram Content Group UK Ltd.
Milton Keynes UK
UKHW010622120423
420030UK00005B/644